*Communication is everything in my business. I am so excited that this book will be an extra tool for those (like me) who need it.*
—*Whitney Reynolds, Emmy nominated PBS talk show host*

*No matter who you are or how you spend your days, Dr. Guinn convincingly argues that communication skills are a nonnegotiable essential to healthy friendships, supervisory relationships, one's leadership capacity, or any professional endeavor. This thoughtful book is teeming with practical tips and wise counsel that I immediately deployed.*
—*Dr. Frank Shushok, President, Roanoke College*

*When you think about the essentials in any subject, you want to be taught by your favorite professor or the best coach you've ever had. Dr. Guinn is both of those in one, and he will help you master the communication essentials in such a way that you'll be amazed at what you learned, how effective you can become, and how much fun it was to do so.*
—*Dr. Dub Oliver, President, Union University*

*Communication Essentials is a special book which has changed the way I communicate and lead. Dr. Guinn's human-centered lessons and applied framework will help many people lead more successful lives.*
—*Dan Peng, Product Manager, Google*

*If How to Win Friends and Influence People was the most famous effective communication skills book of the twentieth century, Communication Essentials will likely be the effective communication classic of our generation. This is the book I wish I had 20 years ago, and I am happy that I have it today. I look forward to sharing it with my coworkers, friends, and*
*family.*
—*Korhan Bircan, Director of Engineering, Meta (Facebook)*

*Dr. Guinn brilliantly coaches his reader to success by simultaneously demonstrating how to effectively communicate through his writing and examples and by providing digestible tips and frameworks. A must-read for anyone seeking greater authenticity, impact, and effectiveness in their abilities to communicate, listen, and engage.*
—*Dr. Kristin Saboe, Psychologist and Senior HR Leader, Boeing*

*In Communication Essentials, Dr. Guinn portrays his charisma and eloquence in words. This book provides a fresh approach to communication frameworks while making the information easy to read. I would recommend this book to anyone looking to improve their communication skills to advance their career.*
—*Rodrigo Landivar, Strategy Consultant, Accenture*

*There are very few books which give you specific actions to follow to improve the most important life skills to accelerate your career in this highly competitive environment. A must-read for everyone who wants to create an edge for themselves in today's fast-changing corporate world.*
—Vikas Prasad, Director of Sales—India, IBM

*Dr. Guinn has given us all a gift in this book—a gift for improved relationships, lasting friendships, a soaring meaningful career, and an overall good life. You will help yourself for life by reading Communication Essentials and absorbing all the advice Dr. Guinn provides.*
—D. F., Senior Technical Program Manager, Meta

*Communication Essentials reads like a friend sitting down with you over coffee, exploring how communication skills influence every part of our lives. Dr. Guinn will help you see communication not as an abstract theory, but as a lifelong journey of better understanding ourselves and others.*
—Dr. Gary Guadagnolo, Director of Research Strategy, EAB

*Communication is a gift to our world. This book flows like a river of joy into all our hearts, showing us how to be kind, kind to others, and kind to ourselves by endorsing communication.*
—Carmen Raicu, Global Head of Africa Sales Operations, Hewlett-Packard

*As a young leader who aspires to inspire my team and deepen my professional network, Communication Essentials has been my golden resource. Highly recommend for those looking to improve life's most essential skill, communication!*
—Justin Brown, Business Manager, Bayer

*Truly essential in continuing the lifelong journey of improving a vital skill (communications) that makes the most challenging conversations in any setting manageable.*
—Afreen Isaac, Supply Demand Management, Apple

*Dr. Guinn is a true master of communication. I'm delighted he is sharing his thinking and methods in this book so that many more can benefit from his guidance.*
—Janet Rhines McIntyre, ECommerce Innovation Marketing Manager, PepsiCo

*This is an excellent book for teaching a framework for effective communication. The principles in this book will help you present your message as effectively as possible.*
—Joe Aviles, Business System Analyst, Google

*Throughout this book, Dr. Guinn provides actionable tips and suggestions on how to become a better communicator as well as real-life success stories. This book is for anyone who wants to become a more highly effective communicator and leader.*
—Dr. Deidra Stephens, Director, University of Texas at Austin

# Also By the Author

*Leaders Communicate:*
*How to Inspire, Influence, and Make an Impact in a Noisy World*

*Winning Connections:*
*Applying Dale Carnegie's Wisdom for Building Relationships*
*and Influence in the 21st Century*

*The Cardinal Playbook:*
*Navigating Graduate Study in Communication Arts*

*The Cardinal Compass:*
*Navigating College and Beyond*

*Communication Essentials:*
*The Tools You Need to Master Every Type of*
*Professional Interaction*

*Adventures in Adulting 2.0:*
*Even More Tales, Trials, and Campfire Conversations*
(with Shannon Guinn)

*Doggy Discovers Gratitude*
(with Shannon Guinn)

# We Relate

*The Art & Science of Meaningful Connections*

BY: TREY GUINN
& SARAH VARGA

Edited by Diane Dempsey

Copyright © 2025. Trey Guinn & Sarah Varga
All rights reserved. No portion of this book may be reproduced, stored in a retrieval system, or transmitted in any form or by any means—electronic, mechanical, photocopy, recording, scanning, or other—except for brief quotations in critical reviews or articles, without the prior written permission of the author and publisher.

11.11.25

The authors may be reached at www.treyguinn.com

ISBN: 9798316371815

Library of Congress Cataloging-in-Publication Data

*This book is dedicated to you—the reader.*

*Thank you for reading and joining us on this learning journey!*

# CONTENTS

Preface — xi

Acknowledgements — xiii

*Part One: The Foundations of Human Connection* — 1

Chapter 1: How Human Relationships Have Evolved Through Time — 5

Chapter 2: Why Relationships Matter — 35

Chapter 3: Identity, Self-Talk, and Intrapersonal Communication — 53

Chapter 4: Relationships and Communication — 71

Chapter 5: How We Build and Maintain Relationships — 93

*Part Two: The Ways We Relate* — 107

Chapter 6: Family and Intergenerational Communication — 111

Chapter 7: Friendship in the Modern World — 129

Chapter 8: The Dynamics of Romantic Relationships — 139

Chapter 9: Communication in the Workplace – Building Meaningful Professional Relationships — 165

*Part Three: Tending Your Relationship Garden* — 177

Chapter 10: When Communication Breaks Down — 181

Chapter 11: Strengthening Relationships Through Emotional Intelligence and Boundaries — 193

Chapter 12: From Tending to Thriving: The Art of Relationship Maintenance — 205

Chapter 13: When Something Ends — 223

| *Part Four: Embracing the Future of Human Connection* | 247 |
| --- | --- |
| Chapter 14: The Evolution and Future of Human Connection | 251 |
| Chapter 15: Building a Relationship Legacy – Cultivating Meaningful Connections Over a Lifetime | 267 |
| Appendices | 283 |
| About the Authors | 291 |

# PREFACE

*Why This Book?*
Relationships are the foundation of our lives. They shape our happiness, influence our mental well-being, and define our experiences.

Yet, despite their importance, few of us are ever explicitly taught how to navigate the complexities of human connection, such as communicating effectively, resolving conflicts with grace, and building bonds that endure.

This book was born from our shared curiosity about what makes relationships thrive and what causes them to falter. Given that we are siblings, our curiosity could be explained by our genetics, shared experiences, or the lifelong conversations centered around family, friendships, love, parenting, and more.

These pages blend some of what we have learned, studied, and taught in relationship research and its real-world application; they are designed to help you explore relationships in all their evolving forms. Whether it's friendship, romantic love, family ties, or workplace dynamics, our ability to connect meaningfully with others is a *skill* that can be learned, refined, and strengthened over time.

*Why This Matters More Than Ever?*
We live in a world of rapid technological advancements and evolving social norms. Social media, remote work, and global connectivity have redefined how we communicate, form bonds, and sustain relationships.

However, these changes have also introduced new challenges, including a rise in loneliness, digital misunderstandings, and the difficulty of maintaining real-world intimacy in a technology-driven society.

Whether you're navigating friendships in the digital age, long-term romantic partnerships, family dynamics, or professional relationships, the insights collected here will help you cultivate deeper, more meaningful connections and bridge the gap between traditional relationship wisdom and modern realities.

*A Note to the Reader.*
This book is not merely a relationship manual but an invitation to reflect, engage, and act. Building strong relationships requires effort, self-awareness, and emotional intelligence. We hope these pages offer insight and encouragement as you navigate the complexities of human connection, allowing you to read, pause, reflect, and engage with the exercises and prompts.

Relationships are not about perfection but about intention. The effort we invest in them shapes the depth of the connections we create.

So, let's begin this journey together.

May this collection of insights serve as a guide, a companion, and a resource as you build relationships that bring meaning, joy, and fulfillment.

# ACKNOWLEDGMENTS

No book is written alone. Behind every word on these pages stands a network of love, encouragement, and support from people who have shaped our journey and made this possible.

First and foremost, our deepest gratitude goes to our parents, spouses, and children. Thank you for loving us so well. Your wisdom, kindness, and unwavering support make every challenge easier and every success more meaningful.

We are especially grateful to our students, colleagues, and mentors, whose insights and conversations continually challenge and sharpen our thinking. Each of you reminds us of the power of communication and connection daily.

Thank you to our friends and community members who have supported us, encouraged our ideas, and reminded us *why* this work matters. Your wisdom and generosity have left an indelible mark on our lives.

Finally, to you, the reader, thank you for picking up this book. Whether you're seeking new insights, fresh perspectives, or practical guidance, we hope these pages serve as a valuable companion on your journey.

Gratefully yours,

- Trey & Sarah

# PART 1:

# THE FOUNDATIONS OF HUMAN CONNECTION

It's 4:15 PM at G12 of a bustling international airport.

To your left, a couple holds hands in silence. The woman leans in close. The man brushes her hair behind her ear. They exchange a few soft words, then a hug that lingers. She walks to the gate slowly. He stays seated, watching her until she disappears.

A toddler runs across the terminal, laughing. His mother chases after him, calling his name. His father catches him by the snack stand and lifts him high. Together, they laugh.

*"Bathroom first,"* the toddler's mother says to him.

The boy cheers for gummy bears.

Two female business professionals stand by a charging station, talking over an open laptop. One points, and the other nods. They smile at something on the screen, then continue typing.

A man yells at the airline desk. *"This is ridiculous!"*

The worker behind the desk responds calmly, *"We're doing what we can, sir."*

He storms off, shaking his head.

A teenage girl lies on her stomach near a wall outlet. She's FaceTiming someone, laughing hard, whispering, *"Don't post that!"* before hanging up.

Two teenage boys whisper and stare at a woman in sunglasses and a hat. One of them takes a sneaky photo.

*"That's her! That's her,"* he says.

You stay where you are, watching it all.

People coming, going, connecting, colliding.

Indeed, in this one moment at this airport, the invisible threads that weave the fabric of our lives together are on display.

Relationships are at the heart of what it means to be human.

Yet, we rarely stop to ask:

*Why do we need a connection in the first place? What is it about relationships that makes them so essential to our well-being? And why do so many people still feel alone in an era of endless digital communication?*

Understanding why relationships matter is crucial before exploring how to build, strengthen, or even repair them. To achieve that, we must revisit the origins of human connection.

*What We'll Explore in This Section:*

## Chapter 1: How Human Relationships Have Evolved Through Time

Explore how human relationships have evolved, from ancient societies to modern social networks, and what our history reveals about the fundamental human need for belonging.

## Chapter 2: Why Relationships Matter

Research shows that relationships are not just a luxury but a biological necessity. This chapter explores why deep human connection remains our most significant source of meaning.

## Chapter 3: Identity, Self-Talk, and Intrapersonal Communication

This chapter delves into self-awareness, identity, and intrapersonal communication, the internal dialogue that shapes our thoughts, emotions, and interactions. We explore how understanding your multifaceted identity can lay the groundwork for healthier, more authentic connections with others.

## Chapter 4: How We Build Healthy Relationships

Why do some relationships feel effortless, while others require careful tending to survive? This chapter helps you unpack the science of relationship-building, including how trust forms and why some relationships last.

## Chapter 5: Relationships and Communication

Explore the verbal and nonverbal cues that shape our interactions and practical strategies for becoming a more effective communicator in every aspect of life. If relationships are the foundation of human connection, communication is the glue that holds them together.

## The Core Idea: Connection is a Skill

We will debunk the myth that relationships should *"Happen naturally."* While chemistry and compatibility play a role, building and sustaining strong relationships is a skill that can be learned, practiced, and improved over time.

By the end of this section, you'll understand why relationships are vital, what makes them succeed or fail, and how communication shapes every connection you have. Most importantly, you'll be equipped with practical tools to create stronger, more fulfilling relationships in your personal and professional life.

So, let's begin our journey!

# Chapter 1:

# How Human Relationships Have Evolved Through Time

*"We lived on farms, then we lived in cities, and now we're going to live on the internet!"*
- *Sean Parker (Justin Timberlake)*
*The Social Network (2010)*

What made humans form relationships with other humans in the first place? Is love universal, or has it changed with time? From the earliest human tribes to the digital world of AI companions, relationships have evolved. However, the need for connection has remained. This story highlights how human relationships have shaped history and been shaped by it.

**But first, a disclaimer:** We do not claim to be historians. And if we were, we certainly wouldn't have the space in this text to include an exhaustive account of human relationship history or the myriad different perspectives that would comprise a comprehensive retelling. We've created a brief overview of the evolution of human relationships and societal structures, enhancing our understanding of today's social landscape and inviting exploration of its origins.

## The Origins of Connection: Prehistory to Ancient Philosophy

Imagine you grew up 10,000 years ago without cities, roads, or a written language. Your world is a small, tight-knit group of about thirty people, mostly relatives, huddled around a fire. Every face is familiar, and trust is essential. You depend on your tribe to hunt, gather, and survive.

In early human societies, family bonds were the foundation of survival. Parents, siblings, and extended kin worked together to gather food and protect one another while raising the next generation. Without these strong family ties, individuals were at risk of isolation and death.

Unlike today, when families are often emotionally driven units, early families were primarily practical alliances, formed out of necessity rather than affection.

Over time, these kinship-based groups established the foundations for inheritance laws, social hierarchies, and the concept of family honor, many of which continue to influence societies today. In this world, relationships are not optional; they are essential to life.

One night, an elder shares a tale in front of the fire, as many gather around:

*"Once, our ancestors could talk to the spirits through the stars."*

The group listens intently. These stories are not just entertainment; they are memory, morality, and identity.

They bind people together in a shared past, reinforcing the trust that holds the tribe together. But as humans grow in number, trust must evolve beyond personal bonds.

## *The First Cities: Trust Beyond Kinship (3000 BCE – 500 BCE)*

Fast forward a few thousand years. Now, you live in Uruk, Mesopotamia (c. 3100 BCE), one of the world's first cities. The world is suddenly vast. Instead of thirty faces, you pass thousands of strangers on the streets. People sell fish, barley, and cloth in a bustling marketplace. Some carried clay tablets with symbols and writing.

While family bonds were dictated by birth, friendships were the first relationships humans actively chose. Aristotle, one of the first thinkers to categorize human connection, believed that friendships of virtue were built on trust, respect, and shared values. These were the friendships that were most enduring and meaningful.

Meanwhile, in China, Confucius included friendship among the five key relationships that structured society, arguing that a virtuous friend could be just as influential as a mentor or ruler.

In many ways, friendships served as a social glue, offering emotional support and shared purpose outside familial duty.

For the first time in human history, relationships extend beyond family. Trade, alliances, and social hierarchies emerge. Hammurabi's Code (c. 1750 BCE) carves the first formal laws into stone, dictating how humans should treat one another:

*"An eye for an eye, a tooth for a tooth."*

This marked a shift. Relationships were no longer governed solely by trust but by contracts and consequences.

Meanwhile, in ancient India (c. 1500 BCE), the Vedas introduced the idea of *dharma,* the moral duty guiding relationships between spouses, rulers, and family members.

In China (c. 500 BCE), Confucius outlines five core human relationships:

1. **Ruler-Subject** (Governance through mutual respect)
2. **Parent-Child** (Filial piety and care)
3. **Husband-Wife** (Defined roles in family structure)
4. **Sibling-Sibling** (Loyalty and duty)
5. **Friend-Friend** (Trust and reciprocity)

At the same time, Greek philosophers Plato and Aristotle explored the meaning of friendship and love. Aristotle classifies friendships into three types:

1. **Utility** (based on mutual benefit)
2. **Pleasure** (based on enjoyment)
3. **Virtue** (based on deep mutual respect)

This is the first time humans have begun to philosophize about the meaning of connection beyond survival or obligation.

This emphasizes that not all relationships were based on kinship or love; some of the most influential bonds in history were those between teachers and students, mentors, and protégés.

In ancient Greece, Socrates mentored Plato, who in turn mentored Aristotle, forming an intellectual lineage that shaped Western thought. In India, guru-disciple relationships formed the backbone of religious and philosophical traditions, with spiritual leaders guiding students in the pursuit of wisdom.

These relationships were not transactional but built on mutual respect, where knowledge was passed down through generations, shaping politics, ethics, and culture.

## *Spiritual and Moral Revolutions: Love, Inclusion, and Ethics (1 CE- 1000 CE)*

Now, imagine walking through the bustling streets of Jerusalem in the 1st century CE. The Roman Empire, a mighty force, controls vast territories, including much of the known world. Although the streets are lined with impressive structures, lives are dictated by the rigid structures of Roman law and societal norms. Class divisions are steep. Roman citizens hold rights and power, while enslaved people are regarded as mere property, without personal freedoms and legal protection. Society is organized on the foundation of hierarchy: Roman law, military conquest, and the ideals of Roman superiority pervade everyday life.

Amidst this backdrop of power and hierarchy, you begin to hear whispers of a man named Jesus of Nazareth. His presence and teachings stir not just curiosity but radical change. Jesus is a revolutionary figure, not in the political sense but in human life's moral and spiritual dimensions.

Jesus speaks of a love that is radically different from anything that was understood before. Instead of love being tied to duty, status, or tribal allegiance, Jesus introduces a new paradigm:

*"Love your enemies. Forgive those who hurt you. Treat others as you wish to be treated."*

In a world where relationships are often transactional, hierarchical, and dictated by social order, Jesus teaches that love should be unconditional and extend beyond those who are like us, those who share our bloodlines, or those of our social class. His message asserts that authentic human relationships are grounded in empathy, forgiveness, and respect for the inherent worth of every individual, no matter their social standing or past actions.

This is no longer love bounded by convention or obligation, but a radical and inclusive love. Jesus' teachings insist that relationships are not governed by power or status, but by the common humanity shared by all. His message profoundly reshapes how humans interact in personal relationships and society. It emphasizes equality, urging people to see the divine in everyone, regardless of their societal position.

As the message of Jesus was carried by his disciples, particularly Paul the Apostle, the message grew into a moral and ethical revolution. Paul's epistles became the first recorded examples of long-distance communication, spreading love, unity, and inclusion far beyond Jerusalem. His writings echo Jesus' call for a new connection between people, which was not based on transactional terms but on mutual respect, compassion, and the understanding that all people deserve dignity and love.

In the centuries that followed, the radical message of Jesus and his apostles shaped how people connect. It transcends not just religious boundaries but also reaches across social, racial, and gender divides. It inspires countless individuals to seek out relationships based on shared values of justice and empathy, forming new communities where love and inclusion are foundational principles.

Jesus' teachings echo through time and are evident today in the actions and philosophies of numerous influential figures and movements. Civil rights leaders like Martin Luther King Jr. drew directly from Jesus' call for love and nonviolence.

His philosophy of peaceful protest and his dream for racial equality were rooted in the belief that all individuals, regardless of race or social standing, should be treated with dignity and respect.

King famously said, "*I have decided to stick with love. Hate is too great a burden to bear,*" a sentiment that mirrors Jesus' teachings on love and forgiveness.

Similarly, Mahatma Gandhi, a champion for India's independence, embraced the principles of nonviolence and forgiveness, inspired by the Sermon on the Mount. Gandhi's concept of "ahimsa" (non-violence) and his insistence on truth and reconciliation reflect the profound influence of Jesus' ethical teachings on human relationships and global movements.

Even today, figures like Mother Teresa, whose life was dedicated to serving the poorest of the poor, embody Jesus' teachings. Mother Teresa's mission of loving those societies is overlooked often, whereas her unwavering compassion for the suffering highlights the ongoing relevance of Jesus' radical love in contemporary society.

Jesus' ethics of love and forgiveness have rippled throughout human history, continuing to inspire social justice campaigns, humanitarian efforts, and moral revolutions. The concept that familial, platonic, or romantic relationships should be built on love and respect rather than power, ownership, or social position becomes central to how people understand and navigate the world.

Jesus introduced a new dimension to human connectivity: the idea that relationships should be rooted in selfless love and that genuine connection requires openness, vulnerability, and the willingness to forgive.

This new way of thinking would influence the evolution of human relationships for millennia, laying the groundwork for the inclusive, interconnected world we continue to navigate today.

Around the same time, Stoic philosophers like Seneca (c. 4 BCE-65 CE) and Cicero (106 BCE-43 BCE) began advocating that relationships should extend far beyond the traditional boundaries of blood ties or close family connections. They argued that human connection and moral duties should not be limited to one's immediate social group but should encompass all of humanity.

This radical shift in thinking was grounded in the Stoic belief in universal reason and natural law. The Stoics argued that all people, regardless of origin or status, share a common human dignity and are bound by the same ethical principles.

For example, Cicero wrote on the nature of justice. His work, *On Duties* (44 BCE), emphasizes that true justice is not confined to nations or peoples but must be extended globally. He proposed that every human being, simply by their humanity, is part of a larger, interconnected moral community.

His philosophical ideas foreshadowed the modern concept of universal human rights, urging that society's moral and political obligations extend to everyone.

Similarly, Seneca argued that one's obligations to others should not be based solely on family ties or proximity but on shared humanity. In his *Letters to Lucilius* (written c. 62-65 CE), Seneca stresses the Stoic belief that the well-being of society depends on individuals embracing a sense of universal brotherhood.

He urged that individuals should feel compassion and responsibility toward all people, especially those suffering, and that these ethical principles transcend familial and social divisions. Seneca's teachings on empathy and justice laid the groundwork for later human rights thinking.

This Stoic view set the stage for later thinkers and movements that would formalize and expand the concept of human rights. Their ideas were a precursor to the modern understanding of equality and justice that emerged during the Enlightenment in the 17th and 18th centuries, ultimately influencing global movements such as the abolition of slavery in the 19th century, women's suffrage in the early 20th century, and the Universal Declaration of Human Rights in 1948. Seneca and Cicero's call for universal moral responsibility remains foundational in contemporary debates about global citizenship, ethics, and the responsibility that humanity has toward its most marginalized members.

Interestingly, by the medieval period, relationships were defined by duty and loyalty. If you were a knight in Europe's feudal system, your allegiance was to your lord and king. Marriage was no longer just a personal arrangement. For some, marriage was a contract or political tool, whereas for others, it was leveraged as an approach to control inheritance.

In medieval Europe, the Church formalized marriage as a sacred union, and noble families arranged marriages to strengthen alliances. Simultaneously, a radical new idea emerged: love could exist outside duty. This idea found its voice in the poetry of courtly love.

Marriages were arranged for power, not love. Yet, something new was emerging, courtly love. In the 12th century, Eleanor of Aquitaine and troubadour poets introduced a new idea: that love should be romantic, passionate, and noble. This marks the beginning of Western culture's obsession with love and devotion.

Nevertheless, medieval life brought economic relationships beyond nobility. Towns and merchant guilds rose, shifting relationships from feudal loyalty to business partnerships.

## *Love, Letters, and Social Codes (1600 CE-1950 CE)*

Now, picture yourself walking through the bustling streets of London in the 1850s. The medieval past is a distant memory. Factories rise above the city, steam trains crisscross continents, and telegrams carry words faster than ever. The world is changing rapidly, but when it comes to love and relationships, one thing remains the same: rules. You cannot simply declare your love to someone. Every interaction is carefully structured, leaving every move scrutinized. Although love does exist, it must follow a script written by tradition and social class.

### The Victorian Age: Love as Duty and Reputation

In Victorian England, marriage was a private affair and a public performance. Every step, from courtship to marriage, is governed by strict social codes. Chaperoned visits ensure no hint of impropriety. Handwritten letters are filled with restrained longing, carefully crafted to reveal just enough emotion, never too much. Strict courtship rituals dictate that even an improper glance can ruin a woman's reputation.

Queen Victoria and Prince Albert are at the heart of this structured world, whose marriage sets the gold standard for relationships, one built on love but also duty and propriety. Their devotion to one another reinforces the idea that marriage should be affectionate and respectful.

But not everyone follows the rules. In candlelit rooms, the Romantic poets such as Lord Byron, John Keats, and Percy Shelley rebel against rigid norms. They write of forbidden passion, heartbreak, and longing, rejecting the idea that love should be confined to duty. Their poetry lays the foundation for modern romantic ideals, inspiring everything from Hollywood films to love songs. Yet love, no matter how poetic, is always shaped by the realities of power and money.

**Love and Economics: The Influence of Karl Marx**
As industrial capitalism spreads, Karl Marx watches and takes note. In *The Communist Manifesto* (1848), he argues that love and marriage are not just personal choices, but economic transactions shaped by class and power.

He sees marriage as an opportunity to control property and inheritance. Who you marry determines wealth, status, and social standing. Marriage also enforces gender roles. Women are primarily dependent on men financially and are treated as economic assets rather than equal partners.

As societies industrialized, relationships within the workplace took on new significance. The medieval world had been defined by feudal bonds between lords and vassals. Still, by the 18th and 19th centuries, laborers and employers formed new economic relationships that were often impersonal but profoundly influential.

Karl Marx argued that, just as marriage had become a financial contract, so too had the relationship between workers and capitalists.

The Industrial Revolution blurred the lines between professional and personal life, with entire families working in factories and social hierarchies forming within the workplace. Even today, our identities are often tied to our careers, and workplace relationships can be as impactful as those within our personal lives.

Marx's ideas would later fuel feminist movements, labor rights debates, and discussions on marriage and equality. As you walk through the streets of London, you see this firsthand. The poor marry for survival and the wealthy for alliances, and love. True, passionate love exists only for those willing to risk social ruin.

*Would you follow your heart, even if it meant giving up everything?*

## Love in Different Cultures Across the World

Beyond Europe, love and marriage take different forms, shaped by tradition, religion, and social expectations.

In China, the Qing Dynasty (1644–1912) followed Confucian ideals, where marriage was about family honor and social harmony. Love may come later, but duty always comes first.

The practice of arranged marriages remains strong, ensuring that unions serve not just individuals but entire family lineages.

In India, marriages are also arranged, often guided by caste, astrology, and family alliances. The concept of swayamvara (choosing one's husband) exists in ancient traditions, but by the 19th century, love marriages remained rare.

British colonial influence began introducing Western ideas, but tradition remained dominant.

Meanwhile, in Japan, the Edo period (1603–1868) saw love as a separate world from marriage.

While noble families arrange marriages for status, love finds an outlet in art, poetry, and even the courtesan culture of the pleasure districts.

The *Tale of Genji*, written centuries ago, continues to shape romantic ideals. Love is fleeting, poetic, and often tragic. It exists everywhere but is always within the boundaries of culture, class, and expectation.

*Would you fight against tradition for love? Or accept the role society assigns you?*

## Love at War: World Wars and Changing Relationships

By the 20th century, everything changed. Wars were ripping people apart. World Wars I and II reshaped not just nations but also relationships. As men left for battle, women stepped into new roles. They worked in factories, ran businesses, and made decisions they could never make.

Marriage was no longer just about duty. It was about survival. Love letters become lifelines, carrying whispered affections across oceans and battlefields. Couples marry in haste, knowing that tomorrow is uncertain. Soldiers hold onto the memory of a lover's face, not knowing if they will ever see them again.

Films like *Casablanca* (1942) capture these fleeting moments, encompassed with intense love, shaped by the uncertainty of war.

When the wars end, the world is different. Women had tasted independence. Men returned, changed by what they had seen. Marriage was no longer the same.

## A New Era of Love and Stability—Or So It Seems

It's 1955, and you are standing in a quiet suburban street. Every house looks the same: neatly manicured lawns, white picket fences, and the hum of a television playing in the background. Inside, families gather around the dinner table.

A father returns home from their 9-to-5 job to find their wife preparing supper and tending to the children. This is the modern ideal. The nuclear family has become the foundation of society, a model reinforced by television shows like *Leave It to Beaver (1957)* and *I Love Lucy (1951)*. Love, marriage, and relationships follow a predictable path: meet the right person, settle down, and start a family.

And yet, beneath the surface, change is brewing. Women are starting to question their roles in the home, and young couples are beginning to resist the rigid expectations of marriage. Across the country, laws that dictate who can and cannot love are being challenged. A cultural revolution is underway. By the 1960s and 1970s, the foundations of love and marriage began to shift.

## The Fight for Racial Equality in Relationships

For centuries, laws have restricted interracial marriage, reinforcing segregation not just in public spaces but in personal relationships. In 1967, Loving v. Virginia changed everything.

The Supreme Court ruled that interracial marriage cannot be illegal, a decision that overturns centuries of racial division in relationships. Love is no longer dictated by race alone. But acceptance is slow, and for many, choosing to love outside social norms has consequences.

*Would you have been willing to fight for love if it meant losing the approval of your community?*

## The Women's Liberation Movement and the Redefinition of Partnership

For decades, marriage has meant dependence for women, financial, legal, and social. A wife's role is clear: caring for the home, raising children, and supporting their husband.

Then comes Betty Friedan's *The Feminine Mystique* (1963), a book that ignites a movement. Women begin to ask questions they were never encouraged to ask before:

*Is this all there is? Should love and marriage define my entire existence?*

By the 1970s, more women entered the workforce, gaining financial independence and shifting the balance of power in relationships. The traditional model of love—where men provide and women nurture—is crumbling.

*If love is no longer about survival or social expectation, what is it?*

**The Sexual Revolution and the Rewriting of Morality.**
Until now, love and sex have been bound tightly to marriage and morality. But in the 1960s, something changed. The *birth control pill* (1960) gives women unprecedented control over their reproductive choices. Sex is no longer just about procreation. It is about pleasure, autonomy, and choice. Premarital sex, once taboo, becomes more accepted. Cohabitation before marriage is rising. Divorce rates increase. LGBTQIA+ relationships begin to gain visibility.

In the movies, love begins to look different. *Bonnie and Clyde* (1967) and *The Graduate* (1967) reject the idea that love must follow society's rules. Passion, rebellion, and unconventional relationships take center stage.

*Would you have embraced this freedom? Or would you have clung to tradition?*

## The Rise of Love in Pop Culture: Hollywood, Music, and Relationship Expectations

In the 1980s and 1990s, love and relationships evolved from traditional, often socially prescribed roles to more complex, individualistic forms of connection. The culture of these decades, shaped by economic change, social movements, and technological advancements, introduced new ideas about how people *should* do relationships. At the heart of this transformation was the media. Movies, television shows, and music redefined love, who deserved it, and what it should feel like.

Movies and television shows of the 1980s and 1990s weren't just entertainment. They were guides to navigating the emotional landscape of relationships. They taught us how to fall in love, maintain relationships, and even break up. These films and shows often depicted relationships as a journey that involved self-discovery, conflict, compromise, and moments of romantic triumph and emotional growth.

John Hughes' iconic teen films like *Sixteen Candles* (1984) and *The Breakfast Club* (1985) tapped into the adolescent desire for emotional validation and belonging. They showed that love wasn't just about romantic conquest but was also about forming meaningful friendships and navigating family dynamics.

In *Sixteen Candles*, Samantha's struggle with being overlooked by her family on her sixteenth birthday revealed a deeply personal story about neglect and the search for love.

Hughes' films normalized feelings of alienation and framed love as a redemptive force that could offer clarity and connection. His portrayals of teen romance set an early benchmark for how love was increasingly seen as a transformative experience that was both romantic and introspective.

In contrast, TV shows like *Cheers* (1982-1993) depicted a more mature view of relationships that blended friendship, romance, and family in a grounded way. The camaraderie and support in the *Cheers* bar weren't limited to the characters' romantic pursuits but also extended to friendships among the regulars. Here, love was shown not only in romantic context but also in platonic friendships, loyalty, and the importance of community.

This was a departure from the idea that love was only about finding "the one." Instead, *Cheers* reflected a more nuanced view: love was in the everyday, the constant support of people who chose to care for one another.

Similarly, *Full House* (1987-1995) introduced a vision of family love that wasn't just about raising children and healing, adaptation, and renewed connections. The show emphasized the importance of emotional support and sharing responsibilities, with a single dad raising his daughters after the tragic loss of his wife. The portrayal of family relationships in *Full House* gave people in the 80s and 90s a template for dealing with challenges, showing that love within the family wasn't just a set of roles to be played out but a deep commitment to emotional nurturing and support.

On the romantic front, films like *When Harry Met Sally* (1989) and *Titanic* (1997) reflected a shift in cultural expectations for romantic love. The relationship between Harry and Sally depicted love as a slow burn, one that grows over time, complicated by friendship but ultimately fulfilling. The film captured the emotional complexity of relationships, showing how they can grow from shared experiences rather than being dictated by idealized notions of love at first sight.

*Titanic* represented a dramatic, sweeping view of love, all-consuming and impossible to resist. It was a vision of love that transcended social class and was defined by passion and sacrifice. For a generation still grappling with the consequences of social change, *Titanic* showed how love could still be epic and timeless, even in a fast-changing world.

However, these portrayals of love also reflect an underlying shift in societal norms. During this period, as gender roles began to evolve and the feminist movement gained more traction, women were depicted more actively in films and TV shows, not just as passive recipients of love but as active participants with their desires, ambitions, and complexities.

*Seinfeld* (1989-1998) introduced an even more cynical approach to relationships, showing that love wasn't always about grand gestures or deep emotional connections. In the world of Seinfeld, romantic relationships were often shallow, transactional, and humorously misguided.

This representation resonated with the growing skepticism about traditional ideals of romance and commitment, questioning whether these ideals were realistic or just constructed fantasies.

Meanwhile, music in the 1980s and 1990s captured love's emotional highs, lows, and complexities. Whitney Houston's *"I Will Always Love You"* (1992) echoed the idea of unconditional love, capturing the bittersweetness of letting go while still holding on to the emotional bond. Her ballad became an anthem for romantic love and love that endures, even in separation.

On the other hand, Tupac's *"Keep Ya Head Up"* (1993) reflected a love deeply rooted in social responsibility, respect, and resilience. His message to young women and marginalized communities was that love should be about strength, not just affection, and that it required self-respect and a sense of solidarity.

In the 1980s and 1990s, love, in all its forms, became a cultural product, shaped by the expectations set by the media. It wasn't just about finding a partner but about showing love for others to see.

Social media had yet to rise, but these decades' media still dictated what was acceptable and desirable in relationships. Hollywood, television, and music pushed the boundaries of what people thought love should look like, whether through idealized romance, the complexities of family dynamics, or the community ties that shaped how we relate.

These media portrayals also gave rise to unrealistic expectations of relationships, suggesting that love, whether familial, platonic, or romantic, should be perfect without struggle. Real-life relationships, however, were messy, complicated, and often imperfect.

But television and film taught audiences that even imperfect relationships were worth pursuing, whether learning how to navigate love in a complex world or embracing the imperfection of family.

The media provided the blueprint for relationships for a generation coming of age in these decades. They reflected the cultural changes that redefined love and connectedness in a rapidly changing world.

By the late 20th century, relationships were not just about social roles but emotional compatibility. The rise of psychology, from John Bowlby's attachment theory to John Gottman's research on relationship dynamics, introduced a new idea: love could be studied, understood, and improved. These studies revealed something sobering: *love isn't just about passion, it's about patterns.* Couples therapy became widespread, self-help books on relationships filled store shelves, and emotional intelligence became just as important as physical attraction.

However, as psychologists uncover the science of connection, something even more significant is about to change everything: the internet.

### *The Digital Age: (Dis)Connection? (2000 – Present)*
Imagine it is the early 2000s. A new way to meet people has emerged. You no longer need to rely on fate, mutual friends, or chance encounters. Now, love is an algorithm.

### The Online Dating Revolution
In the mid-1990s, the advent of online dating websites such as *Match.com (1995), eHarmony (2000),* and *OkCupid (2004)* promised to revolutionize the way people find love and companionship.

These sites introduced the idea of finding your perfect match using algorithms, data, and compatibility tests, offering a more scientific approach to romantic connections. Users filled out detailed questionnaires about their personalities, values, and preferences, and in return, these platforms provided curated matches based on what was most compatible.

This marked the beginning of a new era where relationships were no longer just a matter of chance encounters but could be guided by technology and statistical analysis. Looking back at how people have "dated" across civilization, there are clear parallels with the online dating revolution and stark differences.

Dating has always been about the search for connection, whether driven by societal expectations, family alliances, or personal desires. Arranged marriages were the norm in many cultures, especially during the medieval period and earlier. Families often select partners for their children based on social status, wealth, and familial alliances.

While romantic love wasn't always the primary motivator, relationships had a structure and purpose. Similarly, today's online dating platforms bring together individuals for relationship purposes, though now the emphasis is more on personal choice and romantic compatibility.

Yet, online dating uniquely differs from past dating practices in the level of choice it offers. Unlike earlier practices where families played a pivotal role in matchmaking, modern dating apps allow individuals unprecedented control over who they interact with.

Users can access hundreds or even thousands of potential partners with a few swipes, which contrasts sharply with the more constrained, localized, and community-driven matchmaking that characterized previous eras.

In earlier societies, people primarily married or courted within their own cultural or geographical communities, with less access to broader or more diverse options. In contrast, the global reach of platforms like *Tinder* and *eHarmony* means that a person in New York can meet someone in New Delhi with just a click.

In the past, dating was a slower process involving face-to-face interactions, whether at markets, gatherings, or religious services. These in-person experiences allowed for more profound and often more deliberate connections.

Online dating, however, accelerates the dating process, shifting interactions from real-life meetings to virtual engagements, often centered around brief exchanges through profile pictures and text.

This shift resembles the shift from courtly love to the more transactional forms of romantic arrangements that began to emerge with the Industrial Revolution.

While the Victorian era upheld romantic ideals, the Industrial Age's arrival pushed many relationships into the realm of practicality and economic necessity, which in some ways mirrors today's more goal-oriented online approach to dating.

By 2012, Tinder introduced a new kind of dating based on swipes, instant attraction, and endless choice. Tinder's fast-paced, casual approach made relationships seem even more transactional, reducing them to immediate, often superficial judgments of physical attraction.

This marks a distinct break from earlier dating practices, where romance, courtship, and emotional bonding played a more central role in the early stages of relationships. Yet, the search for connection, whether based on attraction, compatibility, or societal needs remains timeless.

But there's more at play in this online dating culture than just a simple choice between partners. In many ways, the use of dating apps like Tinder has become increasingly gamified, triggering responses in the brain that are very similar to those associated with gambling addiction. When users swipe through profiles, they experience dopamine hits. The brain's reward chemical is activated whenever they get a match or positive feedback.

This creates an addictive instant gratification cycle. Like gambling, where the unpredictability of winning keeps people playing, dating apps offer similar intermittent rewards. Not every swipe leads to a match, but the possibility of a rewarding connection keeps users engaged.

The ease and speed of online dating also feed into this gamified experience. Apps like Tinder can become a source of endless choice and immediate feedback, creating an environment where people engage in "dating as entertainment" rather than focusing on building lasting connections.

However, while technology offered unprecedented options for potential matches, it also raised important questions about the nature of commitment and authenticity in relationships.

The question lingers: *Does having more options make love easier, or does it make commitment harder?*

With so many profiles to choose from, users can feel overwhelmed and often move on to the next swipe before even fully exploring a meaningful connection.

This phenomenon, known as the "paradox of choice," suggests that more options can lead to greater dissatisfaction and indecisiveness, leaving individuals questioning whether they could have found a better match if they'd kept looking.

A troubling aspect of modern digital relationships is the anonymity and ease of access which allows people to engage in deceitful or unethical behavior. This underscores the potential risks of online dating, where emotional and physical intimacy can be manipulated, and trust can easily be violated.

The rise of online dating platforms has also led to concerns about the commodification of love and intimacy. Critics argue that these platforms reduce relationships to transactional exchanges, where people are judged based on superficial attributes such as appearance or initial attraction, rather than deeper qualities like shared values, emotional connection, or compatibility.

In extreme cases, this commodification of relationships may undermine the more profound human need for genuine connection. Despite these challenges, online dating continues to thrive. The convenience of meeting new people without the constraints of geographical location has made it easier for people to find like-minded individuals.

Ultimately, the online dating revolution has brought both opportunities and challenges. On the one hand, it has expanded the possibilities for human connection, making it easier for individuals to meet others outside their immediate social circles. Dating apps also increasingly cater to diverse communities, offering spaces for people with specific interests, identities, or relationship preferences.

On the other hand, it has raised important questions about the nature of love, commitment, and the authenticity of relationships in the digital age. The dating experience has evolved from a local and community-based practice to a fast-paced, global, and often superficial exchange.

However, much like past matchmaking forms, it still revolves around the same timeless quest for companionship, connection, and shared purpose.

## Social Media and the Performance of Love

The introduction of Facebook in 2004 marked a turning point in our understanding of relationships. With its "relationship status" feature, Facebook made love public.

No longer confined to private moments shared between two individuals, love became something that could be curated and broadcast to a broad audience. Couples now could publicly announce their status, often posting intimate updates about their love lives. The ability to express love through photos, status updates, and likes shaped how relationships were experienced and projected.

In many ways, social media platforms like Facebook, Instagram, and Twitter have redefined romantic connections. Now, love isn't just personal; it's a performance for the public, a constant showcase of happiness, longing, and intimacy. You can craft an idealized version of your relationship to gain social approval, but this curated portrayal often lacks depth.

On social media, we curate a performance of love, choosing moments that highlight the joy, the adventures, and the emotional highs, while editing out the mundane or challenging aspects of relationships. This "performance" is shaped by an underlying gamification of social validation, where likes, comments, and shares act as a form of social currency, making us feel more connected. The pressure to present an idealized version of oneself, often curated through carefully chosen photos and profiles, can also foster feelings of inadequacy or inauthenticity.

**Think About It:** Is this performance of intimacy truly reflective of what we experience offline? Or is it an illusion, fostering a desire for validation rather than genuine connection?

Technology's influence on relationships extends beyond romance, impacting friendships and professional connections. Social media platforms enable us to maintain connections across continents, making staying in touch with friends, family, and colleagues easier.

However, these digital friendships can often feel shallow. The pressure to maintain a perfectly curated persona, where every photo and post is an edited version of our life, leaves little room for the complexities of real, face-to-face friendships.

Research suggests that parasocial relationships—the one-sided bonds formed with influencers and celebrities—are becoming a substitute for real-world intimacy. People may feel emotionally connected to a social media influencer or a celebrity, yet the relationship is not reciprocated, leaving the individual feeling emotionally invested but ultimately alone.

These parasocial relationships are particularly concerning in the context of love and intimacy, as they blur the lines between reality and fantasy.

*Virtual intimacy and AI companionship pose new questions.*
AI chatbots like Replika (2023) are increasingly used for romantic companionship, allowing individuals to converse and build relationships with AI that simulate fundamental human interactions. Similarly, virtual reality dating platforms are emerging, where users can interact with digital avatars and form romantic bonds in immersive virtual worlds.

In films like *Her* (2013), where a man forms a romantic relationship with an AI, and in reality, with apps like Replika, we see a future where love is no longer limited to human-to-human interaction.

If technology can simulate love and intimacy, what happens to the genuine human connections we've relied on for centuries? Are we losing the essence of what it means to love? As we move further into an era where relationships can be programmed, we must ask: Will love still be love? Can a simulated relationship provide the same emotional depth as one rooted in genuine human connection? Or are we entering a world where intimacy is increasingly digital and transactional?

The question lingers: Is this evolution of love the next step toward a more connected world? Or does it risk isolating us further as we trade authentic relationships for those that can be programmed, filtered, and edited?

As we explore the increasingly blurred lines between human and artificial connections, the challenge remains to define true intimacy in an age dominated by algorithms and avatars.

*Are we truly more connected, or just more distracted?*

## *Chapter One Reflection Questions*

1. Imagine you lived in a historical period—tribal societies, ancient cities, medieval feudal systems, or the Victorian era. How would your relationships be different? Which era do you think aligns most with your personality and values?
2. Which historical relationship shift do you think had the most significant impact on how we connect today? The invention of written language, the rise of friendship as a chosen relationship, the Industrial Revolution's impact on marriage, or the digital age?
3. Are there past relationship traditions that should make a comeback? Arranged marriages over online dating? Handwritten letters instead of texting?
4. The rise of psychology introduced the idea that we should "study" relationships. Do you think this has helped people create healthier relationships, or has it led to overanalyzing love over simply experiencing it?
5. Do you think social media has enhanced or weakened human connection? Are people more connected than ever or lonelier than before?
6. AI companions, virtual relationships, and parasocial bonds with influencers are growing. Are these new forms of connection a solution to loneliness or a barrier to intimacy? Would you trust an algorithm to find a partner or a best friend? Why or why not?
7. If we are moving toward a world where love and friendship can be "programmed" through AI, would you choose human relationships, with all their unpredictability and flaws? Why or why not?

## *Chapter One Challenges*

1. The Digital Detox Experiment: For one day, try disconnecting from social media and texting, and instead. Call a friend instead of sending a text. Handwrite a letter to someone you care about. Spend time with someone in person without checking your phone. Reflect: Did the lack of digital communication make you feel more present? More disconnected?
2. Love & Friendship Throughout History: Debate & Discuss: In a group or with a partner, choose one of the following debate topics and take opposite sides:
   * Arranged Marriages vs. Modern Dating – Did historical matchmaking create stronger marriages than today's self-selected relationships?
   * Courtly Love vs. Practical Love – Is passion or partnership more important in a long-term relationship?
   * Digital Friendships vs. In-person Friendships – Can online friendships be as deep and meaningful as face-to-face ones?
   * AI Companionship vs. Human Connection – If an AI could perfectly understand you, would you choose it over a human relationship?
3. Relationship Forecast Discussion: What Will Love & Friendship Look Like in 100 Years? Imagine you've traveled 100 years into the future. What do relationships look like? Is marriage still common, or has it evolved into short-term contracts? Do people still meet in person, or is dating and friendship entirely virtual? Are AI companions a normal part of life? Have new types of relationships emerged?

… WE RELATE

# Chapter 2:

# Why Relationships Matter

*"Connection is why we're here; it is what gives purpose and meaning to our lives."*
     - Brené Brown

At the heart of human history is one undeniable truth: we need each other. From the earliest tribal bonds to the digital connections of today, relationships have shaped our survival, cultures, and sense of self. But beyond the historical shifts explored in the previous chapter, one big question remains.

**Why Do We Need Each Other?**
It's easy to assume that romantic, familial, or professional relationships are merely a product of culture and tradition. But what if they're something more? What if our drive to connect is woven into our biology, influencing our emotions and physical and mental well-being?

Modern life presents a paradox: we are more connected than ever, yet loneliness is at an all-time high. Social media gives us instant access to thousands of people, yet many still feel unseen.

The COVID-19 pandemic forced us to reckon with isolation in ways we never had before, making it clear that virtual interactions, while useful, can never fully replace the richness of in-person connection.

And there's a reason for that.

Loneliness isn't just an emotion. It's a biological warning sign. Research shows that chronic loneliness is as damaging to health as smoking 15 cigarettes a day. Human connection doesn't just shape our happiness. It influences our success, resilience, and even our longevity.

*So, what went wrong? If we have more communication methods than any generation before us, why do so many people feel alone?*

And more importantly, how can we reclaim the deep, meaningful connections that make life truly fulfilling?

## What *Friends*, *Into the Wild*, the Pandemic, and Nelson Mandela Teach Us About Connection

Sometimes, the best lessons about relationships don't come from textbooks—they come from *stories*. From a sitcom about six friends in a coffee shop to a young man who sought solitude in the wilderness, these stories reveal something universal: we are wired for connection.

As you read, put yourself in the driver's seat. What would you have done in these situations? How do these stories reflect your own experiences with relationships?

## Why We Loved *Friends*

For ten seasons, *Friends* followed the lives of Monica, Ross, Rachel, Chandler, Joey, and Phoebe as they navigated love, careers, and the chaos of adulthood. The show wasn't groundbreaking because of its plot. The relationships are what made it relatable and timeless.

At its core, *Friends* wasn't just about jokes or romance. The show was about having a chosen family. It showed us that deep, meaningful friendships could be as powerful as romantic relationships or family bonds. It reminded us that no matter how unpredictable life can be, having people who truly "get" you makes all the difference.

Imagine your life as a sitcom. Who are the main characters in your story? What roles do they play—are they the supportive friend, the chaotic adventurer, the voice of reason? How do these relationships shape your life?

**Think About It:** Picture your own life. Who is your "Friends" group? The people who celebrate your wins, pick you up when you fall, and make even the worst days bearable?

### *Into the Wild* and Extreme Solitude

Imagine leaving everything behind, including your phone, family, and friends, to set off alone into the wilderness. You will be free of distractions, obligations, and expectations. It will be just you, surviving on your own.

This wasn't just an idea for Christopher McCandless. It was his reality. His story, which is depicted in *Into the Wild*, follows his journey as he abandons society in search of ultimate freedom.

No possessions, no relationships—just nature and self-reliance. But as the months passed, something shifted. In the pages of his journal, he wrote a final revelation:

*"Happiness is only real when shared."*

He had achieved what so many people think they want—total independence. Yet, in his solitude, he realized that life's greatest moments mean little if there's no one to share them with.

Now, think about your happiest memories. Were these moments spent alone, or were they made meaningful by the people around you?

Would that road trip, late-night conversation, or moment of achievement feel the same if no one were there to experience it with you?

**Think About It:** If you could relive one of your happiest moments, who would you want to share it with? Why?

## The Pandemic's Lesson on Isolation

In 2020, the world was forced into sudden isolation. Streets emptied, offices shut down, and relationships moved entirely online for many.

At first, it may have seemed manageable to do life via Zoom and social media. But as the months dragged on, a more profound truth became painfully clear: digital connections can never fully replace face-to-face interaction.

Studies showed that prolonged isolation during the pandemic led to increased rates of depression, anxiety, and cognitive decline (Killgore et al., 2020). Even introverts who enjoyed alone time longed for real, human presence.

**Think About It:** During COVID, what did you miss most? Was it the simple comfort of sitting next to a friend? Or was it the energy of a crowded café? Perhaps, it may have been the ability to hug someone without worry?

If nothing else, the pandemic was a stark reminder that we don't just want connection. We *need* a connection. If another period of social isolation were to happen, what steps would you take to stay emotionally connected?

**Nelson Mandela: Connection as a Tool for Change**
While COVID-19 lockdowns were a very real and difficult time for many of us, imagine being wrongfully locked away for 27 years. Nelson Mandela's imprisonment could have hardened him.

He could have emerged bitter, resentful, and unwilling to forgive those who had taken so much from him. Instead, he used relationships as a tool for change.

Even within the prison walls, Mandela built bridges where others saw barriers. He befriended his correctional officers, understanding that human connection could shape history even in the most divided circumstances.

When he was finally released, his ability to foster reconciliation helped end apartheid in South Africa.

Mandela's story proves that relationships aren't just about personal happiness. Relationships have the power to change the world.

**Think About It:** Have you ever built a connection with someone completely different from you? Maybe a coworker with opposing views, a stranger from another culture, or even someone you initially disliked? What did that connection teach you?

## We Are Wired for Connection
By now, one truth is clear: human connection is not just a luxury, it's a necessity. From Christopher McCandless's realization in the Alaskan wilderness to how *Friends* has resonated across generations to our own lived experiences in the pandemic, our need for relationships is undeniable.

Even history's greatest leaders, like Nelson Mandela, understood that connection wasn't just personal. It was powerful enough to change the world. But *why* do we need people so desperately? Why does loneliness feel like pain, while deep relationships give life meaning? The answer lies in science.

Our instincts for connection go far beyond emotions—they are wired into our biology. From our ancestors' survival strategies to modern psychological research, science shows that relationships impact everything—our health, success, even how long we live.

*So, let's take a deeper dive.* Why do our brains prioritize social bonds? How does connection influence our well-being? And what happens—biologically, psychologically, and emotionally—when we lack meaningful relationships?

## The Science Behind Human Relationships
Imagine you're stranded on a deserted island. At first, it might seem freeing—no obligations, no one to judge you, no drama. But as the days pass, a new kind of discomfort sets in.

The silence becomes unbearable, and the lack of human contact is unsettling. You begin talking to yourself, or maybe even to a volleyball like Tom Hanks' character in *Cast Away*.

This isn't just boredom—it's biology. Our need for connection isn't a preference; it's a survival mechanism. Evolutionary psychology suggests that human intelligence evolved primarily to manage social relationships (Dunbar, 1998).

Our ancestors who formed strong social bonds had a higher chance of survival—they hunted together, protected each other, and passed down knowledge. Those who were isolated were more vulnerable to danger and had fewer opportunities to reproduce, meaning their genes faded out over time.

But even in today's world, where survival is less about fighting off predators and more about navigating work, relationships, and stress, the biological consequences of isolation remain severe.

Your brain sees social disconnection as a threat. Loneliness triggers a stress response—your body releases cortisol, the hormone responsible for fight-or-flight reactions. Chronic loneliness leads to inflammation and over time can even weaken the immune system.

Studies show that long-term isolation shrinks the brain (Cacioppo & Cacioppo, 2018), affecting memory, decision-making, and emotional regulation.

**Think About It:** Think about a time when you felt isolated—maybe moving to a new city or starting a new job. How did it affect your mood, energy, or well-being?

## How Relationships Change Your Brain
What happens inside your brain when you experience a deep connection with someone?

### *1. The Oxytocin Effect – "Love & Trust Hormone"*
Oxytocin is a powerful neurochemical released when we bond with others. It can be triggered by anything from a hug to an intimate conversation, reinforcing feelings of safety and trust.

Research shows higher oxytocin levels are linked to lower stress and better emotional resilience (Carter, 2014). Lack of oxytocin has been associated with increased social anxiety and difficulty trusting others. People in healthy romantic or friendship-based relationships produce more oxytocin, reducing the risk of depression.

### *2. Mirror Neurons – The Key to Empathy*
Have you ever winced when you saw someone else get hurt? That's mirror neurons at work. They allow us to feel what others feel. Mirror neurons explain why we cringe at awkward situations in TV shows, how we feel connected to fictional characters as if they were real, and why face-to-face interactions are richer than digital conversations; we subconsciously pick up on micro-expressions, tone, and body language that text messages can't convey.

### *3. The Loneliness-Brain Shrinkage Effect*
Loneliness is not just a feeling — it can physically change the brain. Studies using MRI scans show long-term loneliness physically reduces brain volume, particularly in areas linked to emotional regulation and decision-making (Cacioppo & Cacioppo, 2018). A lack of interaction raises the risk of cognitive decline and dementia in older adults (Wilson et al., 2007).

**Think About It:** In the previous chapter, we offered a challenge of a digital detox—no texting, no social media. Chances are that if you tried it, you recognized some benefits. But imagine adding to the challenge, no face-to-face conversations or human interaction, for that matter. How would that make you feel? Do you find yourself craving connection in small ways—eye contact, casual conversation, or even scrolling social media for interaction? How does this compare to days you've had deep conversations or meaningful human interactions?

**The Role of Relationships in Career and Success**
Anthropologist Robin Dunbar suggests that humans can only maintain about 150 meaningful social relationships simultaneously. But how does this translate to modern success?

Sociologist Mark Granovetter's *"Strength of Weak Ties" theory (1973)* suggests that most career opportunities come from acquaintances, not close friends. His work says that even loose social connections can introduce you to new ideas, industries, and mentors, and that expanding your network likely leads to greater success than simply deepening existing close relationships.

A study from the National Bureau of Economic Research *(Gee et al., 2017)* found that people with diverse social networks earn higher salaries and have better career mobility. Knowing many different types of people, from mentors to coworkers, can be just as valuable as maintaining deep relationships with a few.

The lesson is that your network equals your opportunities. In addition to positively influencing our personal happiness, networking and relating with others significantly impact our professional success.

## Self-Determination Theory: Relationships, Autonomy, and Growth

While relationships are essential, they are not the only factor in personal fulfillment. Self-Determination Theory (Ryan & Deci, 2000) argues that humans thrive when three psychological needs are met:

1. **Autonomy** – Feeling in control of your own life.
2. **Competence** – Feeling effective in what you do.
3. **Relatedness** – Feeling connected to others.

This matters for several reasons. Consider that if you have deep relationships but lack autonomy (e.g., feeling trapped in a toxic relationship), you may lack a sense of personal fulfillment. Or, if you have strong friendships but no sense of competence (e.g., struggling in your career), your overall happiness and satisfaction may be compromised.

Healthy relationships provide connection but also leave room for autonomy and growth. You don't need to be constantly surrounded by people to feel fulfilled, but investing in the right ones can make all the difference.

All this to say, balancing relationships with personal growth is key—one should enhance the other, not replace it.

**Think About It:** How do your closest relationships support—or hinder—your autonomy and personal growth?

## The Social Media Paradox

Picture this: you've got hundreds of followers, your group chat is blowing up, and you're maintaining streaks like a pro. And yet, deep down, you feel strangely... disconnected. Sound familiar?

We live in a time of nonstop digital interaction. Messages, likes, comments, and DMs are just a tap away. But despite all these connections, rates of loneliness, anxiety, and depression are at an all-time high. Why is it that with more "friends" than ever, we often feel more alone?

Psychologist and author Sherry Turkle describes this tension in her book *Alone Together* (2011). She explains that even though we have more ways to communicate, we've lost the richness of real connection. Turkle argues that while digital connections allow us to stay in touch, they create an illusion of intimacy. Social media offers the appearance of closeness but often leaves individuals feeling more isolated and disconnected.

This idea is supported by Erving Goffman's theory of self-presentation (1959), which suggests that people act in ways that influence how others perceive them, much like actors on a stage.

Digital communication is convenient, but it can also be shallow. We send quick texts instead of having long talks, respond with emojis instead of emotions, and scroll through someone's perfectly filtered life without ever checking in. It's like we're all standing in each other's digital lobbies but rarely stepping inside to sit down and really talk.

This isn't just theory; it's backed by research. A 2018 study by Jean Twenge and colleagues found that heavy social media users reported significantly higher levels of loneliness, anxiety, and depression than people who prioritized face-to-face time. Watching someone's Instagram story may feel like you're part of their world, but it's a passive experience. You're observing, not connecting. It's the difference between watching a party and being invited in.

This raises an important question: Do your online interactions enhance your real-life relationships or replace them? How do you feel after spending hours scrolling compared to how you feel after a good, in-person conversation? If you're like most people, the difference is noticeable.

And it matters more than we often realize. Relationships aren't just nice additions to our lives but biologically essential.

As we have seen, our brains are wired to connect, and prolonged isolation can change how they function. Strong social bonds improve not just emotional well-being but also physical health, resilience, and even career success. Deep, meaningful friendships offer support that likes and comments can't replicate.

And yet, it's not about how many people you know—it's about how deeply you are known. Ten surface-level connections will never give you what one truly present, supportive friend can offer.

**Think About It:** Who are your three most important people right now? Why those three? How often do you engage in honest, deep conversation that is not just a quick *"how's it going"* but a meaningful back-and-forth that sticks with you?

And overall, do you feel connected... or disconnected in your day-to-day life? And if you're feeling a bit disconnected, you're not alone.

Sometimes the most significant barriers to connection are invisible—fear of rejection, past hurt, social exhaustion, or the temptation to settle for surface-level interactions. It's easier to ghost someone than to say, *"Hey, I need you."*

It's easier to scroll than to share.

But what if we pushed through that discomfort? What if we chose to show up, even when it's awkward? What if we dared to be present?

Let's end with a scenario to think about. Imagine you've just moved to a brand-new city. You don't know anyone. You've got work and your phone, but no in-person friends yet. What do you do first to start building real relationships—not just a collection of new followers, but actual community?

There's no one right answer. Maybe you'd join a club, go to a church, or ask someone to grab coffee. Maybe you'd sign up for a group run or a trivia night. The important thing is to start. Because the truth is, meaningful connection takes time, effort, and sometimes a little bit of bravery. But it's always, *always* worth it.

## You Need Relationships

At the end of our lives, we won't measure success by our number of followers, net worth, or achievements—we'll measure it by the meaningful relationships we built.

The science is clear: connection isn't a luxury; it's a survival need. And yet, in a world that pulls us in a thousand directions, we often take our relationships for granted.

## *Chapter Two Reflection Questions*

1. Do your online interactions bring you closer to people—or do they sometimes keep you at a distance? Think about the last time you spent an hour on your phone. Did it make you feel energized, seen, and connected? Or did it leave you feeling left out, empty, or even anxious?
2. When was the last time you had a meaningful, in-person conversation? Not just a passing "what's up," but a real conversation where you felt known. What made it meaningful? How did you feel afterward?
3. What do you think gets in the way of deeper relationships? Is it fear? Busyness? Past experiences? Or maybe just the comfort of staying in surface-level spaces where you don't have to be vulnerable?
4. Consider your professional connections. Are you relying too much on a small inner circle? How could you expand your network meaningfully?
5. Do you feel more connected or disconnected in your daily life? It's okay if the answer surprises you. This is a space for honest reflection, not judgment. The goal isn't perfection—it's awareness.

## *Chapter Two Challenges*

1. Make a Real Connection. Reach out to someone you care about and ask to meet up in person. Coffee, lunch, a walk—whatever works. Put away your phone and be fully present. Let the conversation go deeper than usual.
2. Curate Your Feed. Take 10 minutes to scroll through your social media and unfollow or mute accounts that make you feel drained, insecure, or disconnected. Follow people who inspire real reflection or bring joy—and notice the shift.
3. Journal About Disconnection. Write one page about a time you felt lonely—even when surrounded by people (or notifications). What was missing? What do you need in moments like that? This isn't just cathartic—it's clarifying.
4. Start a Meaningful Conversation. Ask someone a question that goes beyond the usual:
"What's something that's been on your mind lately?"
"What do you wish people understood about you?"
You might be surprised how ready people are to go deeper when given the chance.
5. Join Something New. If you're feeling disconnected, take one brave step toward community. Go to a new group, club, church, or event—somewhere people gather in real life. You don't have to make your best friend on day one. Just show up.

## *Next Up: The Self in Relationships*

Throughout history, we've seen how relationships shape our survival, happiness, and success. From ancient tribes to modern digital networks, our need for connection is undeniable. But what if the key to forming deeper, more meaningful relationships doesn't start with others—it starts with us?

Before we can truly understand and connect with the people around us, we must ask: Who am I?

Self-awareness is the foundation of all relationships. The way we see ourselves affects how we communicate, how we interpret the world, and how we navigate friendships, family dynamics, and professional interactions. Yet, identity is not static. It shifts with experience, feedback, and even our own internal dialogue.

In this next chapter, we turn inward. We'll explore how self-perception shapes our interactions, why our inner voice matters, and how understanding ourselves allows us to build stronger, more authentic relationships with others.

Let's begin the journey of self-awareness.

## WE RELATE

# Chapter 3:

# Identity, Self-Talk, and Intrapersonal Communication

*"Knowing yourself is the beginning of all wisdom."*
— *Aristotle*

**Who Am I, Really?**
At first, this might seem like a simple question. You might respond with your name, your job, your major, or your hometown. But if you strip those labels away, what remains? Are you the person you believe yourself to be? Or are you shaped by how others see you? And if the way you view yourself changes over time, what does that say about identity—do we create it, or does it create us?

Most of us assume that identity is fixed—that our personality, values, and core traits remain stable. But self-awareness is a constant negotiation between who we think we are, how others perceive us, and who we want to become. Every experience, conversation, and relationship shapes us, often in ways we don't immediately recognize.

And at the center of it all is our inner voice—the constant dialogue running in our minds. This internal conversation influences our confidence, our decisions, and how we interact with others.

Yet, self-awareness isn't just about looking inward—it's also about how we engage with the world and the feedback we receive. What does it truly mean to "know yourself"?

Is self-awareness something we earn through experience over time, a deliberate choice we make, or something shaped and even imposed by the world around us?

These are big questions—ones that don't have quick answers. To explore them, we'll look at the science behind self-awareness and how our brains actually form identity and self-perception. We'll consider the role of self-talk and how the way we speak to ourselves influences everything from our confidence to our mental health. We'll also explore how identity isn't fixed, but shifts over time—and how embracing that fluidity can lead to healthier relationships and wiser decisions. Finally, we'll reflect on the idea of divine communication and how spiritual connection can shape our understanding of who we are at the deepest level.

Before we dive in, let's take a moment to look at how self-awareness shows up in some of the stories we know and love—because sometimes, fiction has a way of holding a mirror up to real life.

### *Using Media and Real-Life Experiences to Learn about Self-Understanding*

We often think we know ourselves—until something forces us to question it. Pop culture is filled with characters on self-discovery journeys, struggling with who they are, who they're expected to be, and how others perceive them. Sometimes, their biggest revelations come not from introspection, but from interactions with others.

## The Many Versions of You

Imagine waking up and realizing that, in another universe, you are someone entirely different.

In *Everything Everywhere All at Once*, Evelyn Wang sees countless versions of herself—each shaped by different choices. She asks herself: *Who am I, really? Am I the person I am now or the person I could have been.*

Her journey highlights something psychologists call self-concept fluidity—the idea that identity is not a rigid, unchanging trait, but something that evolves based on experience and perspective.

*"You are not unlovable. There is always something to love."* – Waymond Wang, *Everything Everywhere All at Once*

That's a powerful idea. It suggests that self-awareness isn't just about understanding *who* we are—it's also about understanding *who we have the potential to be*.

**Think About It:** If you had chosen a different major, moved to a different city, or made a different career choice, how different would you be? Would you still feel like "yourself"?

## The Social Mirror: How Others Shape Who We Are

While self-awareness might feel like an internal journey, it's shaped by the world around us. We don't just decide who we are—we constantly interpret feedback from others.

**The Looking-Glass Self: Seeing Ourselves Through Others' Eyes.** Sociologist Charles Cooley (1902) introduced the concept of the looking-glass self—the idea that our self-image is shaped by how we *think* others perceive us.

In other words, we don't just define ourselves—we construct our identity based on social feedback. This can be empowering, but it can also create distortions.

Have you ever been told something about yourself that *didn't* align with how you saw yourself? Maybe a friend said, *"You always seem so confident,"* when internally, you've struggled with self-doubt. Or maybe you've been labeled as *shy* or *outspoken*, even though you don't fully identify with those traits. The dissonance can be unsettling, leading us to ask: *Am I who I think I am, or am I who others perceive me to be?*

### *Fleabag* – The Stories We Tell Ourselves
In *Fleabag*, the protagonist constantly breaks the fourth wall, speaking directly to the audience as if she's in control of her own story. But over time, we realize something: her asides aren't just clever—they're a shield. She's not talking to us—she's talking to herself, avoiding the reality of her pain. This is an example of **defensive self-talk**; a mechanism we all use to avoid uncomfortable truths. We might tell ourselves, *I don't care what people think* when deep down, we do. Or we say, *I'm fine on my own* when we're actually craving connection.

*"Either everyone feels like this a little bit and they're just not talking about it, or I am completely alone."* – Fleabag

**Think About It:** Do you speak to yourself in a way that builds you up, or do you deflect and protect yourself from uncomfortable truths?

## How Your Inner Voice Shapes Your Reality
Now, let's turn inward. If you had to narrate your inner dialogue for a day, what would it sound like? Would it be kind, encouraging, and confident? Or would it be critical, doubting, and anxious?

Psychologists divide self-talk, also called intrapersonal communication, into two main categories. Positive self-talk is about encouraging, solution-oriented inner dialogue, whereas negative self-talk is about self-critical, anxious, or limiting beliefs.

Dr. Shad Helmstetter, in his book *What to Say When You Talk to Yourself*, argues that the way we speak to ourselves directly influences our self-esteem, motivation, and even success.

Consider the self-fulfilling prophecy—a psychological phenomenon where our beliefs shape our reality. If you constantly tell yourself, *I'm terrible at public speaking*, your brain will work to make that belief true. But if you shift your self-talk to *I'm improving at public speaking*, you create space for growth.

**Think About It:** What's one self-limiting belief you've repeated to yourself? What if you reframed it?

## Moana – Rewriting the Narrative
Moana's journey is not just about sailing beyond the reef—it's about answering the question: *Am I just who my family expects me to be, or am I something more?*

At first, her self-talk is full of doubt: *What if I'm not the right person to lead? What if I fail?* But as she gains experience, her inner dialogue shifts. She no longer questions if she is meant to follow her heart—she declares it: *I am Moana.*

This mirrors psychologist Carol Dweck's **growth mindset theory**, which argues that shifting from a *fixed mindset* (*I'm either good or bad at something*) to a *growth mindset* (*I can improve through effort*) leads to greater success and resilience.

**Think About It:** Before we move forward, take a moment to reflect—how often does your self-perception align with how others see you? What's one belief about yourself that you've outgrown—but still hold onto? How does your inner dialogue shape the way you navigate challenges?

In the next section, we'll explore the science behind self-awareness, how our brains construct identity, and why our inner voice is one of the most powerful tools we have.

### When Blind Spots Are Revealed

Think back to a time when someone gave you feedback that completely surprised you. Maybe a friend told you that you interrupt people more than you realized. Maybe a professor pointed out that you downplay your intelligence. Maybe a mentor saw leadership potential in you before you saw it in yourself.

For Trey, that moment came in graduate school. He always believed he was confident in class discussions—until one day, a professor he deeply respected pulled him aside.

"Trey," he said, "you always have insightful thoughts, but sometimes, you hesitate to speak up. It's almost like you're holding back, as if you're not convinced your contributions are valuable." Caught off guard, Trey had never seen himself as hesitant. But as he reflected, he realized—his professor was right. He second-guessed his ideas, waiting for the perfect way to phrase them before speaking. That hesitation had become an unconscious pattern, shaping how he presented himself to others.

It was a blind spot—an aspect of Trey's identity that others could see, but he had never recognized; and once he became aware of it, he could work on it.

Self-awareness isn't just about introspection. It's about listening when the world holds up a mirror.

### How Well Do You Know Yourself?
The truth is, we all have blind spots. But self-awareness isn't just about discovering weaknesses—it's about understanding the full picture of who we are, including our strengths, habits, and patterns. Let's put this to the test with an interactive quiz.

### How Self-Aware Are You?
1. When receiving feedback, I...
    - A) Welcome it and reflect on how I can improve.
    - B) Feel defensive but try to process it later.
    - C) Get frustrated and ignore it.

2. When I talk to myself, my inner dialogue is mostly...
    - A) Encouraging and solution-oriented.
    - B) A mix of self-doubt and self-motivation.
    - C) Critical and negative.

3. When I make a mistake, I usually...
    - A) Learn from it and move forward.
    - B) Dwell on it for a while before moving on.
    - C) Feel like a failure.

4. How well do I understand how others perceive me?
    - A) Very well—I regularly seek feedback.
    - B) Somewhat—I get feedback occasionally but don't always act on it.
    - C) Not well—I rarely ask for or listen to feedback.

If you have mostly A's: You have strong self-awareness and a healthy self-dialogue. Mostly B's: You have some self-awareness but might benefit from deeper self-reflection. Mostly C's: You may struggle with self-awareness and self-talk—consider practicing self-reflection exercises.

The truth is that even the most successful people have wrestled with self-doubt. The key is learning how to recognize it—and reframe it. Let's take a look at two well-known women who have openly shared their struggles with self-doubt—and how they've worked to overcome it.

### Oprah Winfrey's Journey to Self-Awareness

Oprah Winfrey, one of the most influential media figures of all time, has openly spoken about her early struggles with impostor syndrome—the persistent feeling that she wasn't as competent as people believed.

Early in her career, despite her talent and intelligence, she worried she wasn't qualified enough to be in certain spaces. But over time, she learned the power of self-talk and self-reflection. Her breakthrough came when she realized: "You become what you believe." The way she talked to herself mattered just as much as the way the world perceived her. Oprah's story reminds us that self-awareness isn't about achieving certainty—it's about committing to growth.

### Michelle Obama's Struggle with Self-Doubt

Even Michelle Obama, despite her immense success, has spoken publicly about experiencing impostor syndrome. In her memoir *Becoming*, she describes moments of doubt, even while attending Princeton or standing alongside world leaders. Her turning point? Feedback and reframing. By recognizing that her self-doubt wasn't rooted in reality, she shifted her inner dialogue. She stopped asking, "Am I good enough?" and started asking, "What unique value do I bring?"

**Think About It:** Have you ever felt like an impostor in a role you've earned? What feedback or experiences helped you shift that perspective?

## The Science of Self-Awareness and Intrapersonal Communication

Self-awareness isn't just a feel-good concept—it has been studied extensively in psychology. One of the most useful models for understanding self-awareness is The Johari Window.

## The Johari Window: The Different Sides of Yourself.

Developed by psychologists Joseph Luft and Harrington Ingham, the Johari Window is a tool that helps us map different dimensions of self-awareness.

| Quadrant | Description | Example |
|---|---|---|
| Open Self | The aspects of yourself that you and others are aware of. | You know you're a good leader, and others recognize it too. |
| Hidden Self | The aspects of yourself that you know but keep private. | You feel insecure about your intelligence but never voice it. |
| Blind Self | The aspects of yourself that others see, but you don't recognize. | A friend points out that you interrupt people a lot, but you were unaware. |
| Unknown Self | The aspects of yourself that neither you nor others have discovered. | A hidden talent or reaction that emerges in unexpected situations. |

What does this mean for you? If you want greater confidence, work on moving parts of your *Hidden Self* into the *Open Self* by sharing more with trusted people. If you want to grow, invite feedback that reveals aspects of your *Blind Self*. If you want to explore your potential, try new experiences that push you outside your comfort zone— you may discover something in your Unknown Self.

## Communicating with the Divine – Faith, Spirituality, and the Sacred Conversation

At some point in life, many people find themselves whispering a prayer, seeking guidance from the universe, or silently hoping for a sign. Whether in times of joy, desperation, gratitude, or uncertainty, the act of communicating with the divine is one of the oldest and most universal human experiences.

But what does it mean to "speak" with the divine? Is prayer a monologue, or can it be a conversation? And how do people across cultures and faith traditions engage in this sacred dialogue?

In this section, we'll explore the many ways people communicate with the divine, the psychological and emotional impact of spiritual connection, and how faith-based communication shapes human relationships. But first, let's consider media.

## Bruce Almighty – When God Talks Back

In *Bruce Almighty*, Jim Carrey's character, Bruce, struggles with faith and frustration, constantly questioning why God isn't responding to his prayers. Then, after a divine encounter with Morgan Freeman (God), Bruce learns that communication with the divine isn't always about hearing an audible voice. Sometimes, it's about seeing signs, paying attention to the world around us, and reflecting on our own choices.

This comedic yet profound take on spirituality highlights a common question: Is God silent, or are we just not listening in the right way?

## Joan of Arcadia – God Speaks in Unexpected Ways

The TV show *Joan of Arcadia* follows a teenage girl who begins to receive direct messages from God, appearing to her in various human forms. While God never forces Joan's choices, these encounters push her to think deeper, see others with compassion, and take responsibility for her actions.

This show reflects the idea that divine communication doesn't always come in dramatic revelations—it often comes in quiet nudges, everyday interactions, and moments of clarity.

## Finding Meaning in Unexpected Moments

A friend once shared about a moment in her life when she felt completely lost—her career was uncertain, a relationship had ended, and she felt spiritually disconnected. One night, she sat in her car and simply said, "God, if You're there, I need a sign." A few minutes later, a song came on the radio with lyrics that spoke directly to what she was feeling.

Was it coincidence? Maybe. But to her, it felt like a divine response—a small but powerful reminder that she wasn't alone.

**Think About It:** Have you ever felt like you received a sign, an answer, or a sense of peace after praying or reflecting?

## Why Do Humans Seek Spiritual Connection?

For centuries, psychologists, theologians, and philosophers have wrestled with the question of why humans crave a connection with something greater than themselves. The need for divine communication seems to be woven into the fabric of our humanity.

At its core, spiritual connection offers a grounding force—something to cling to when the world feels chaotic. Research shows that engaging in spiritual practices like prayer and meditation can regulate our emotions by activating brain regions associated with peace and resilience. This isn't just about "feeling better"—it's about being able to face life's complexities with a steadier heart.

Beyond that, spirituality gives us tools for meaning-making. In moments of grief, loss, or even in the monotony of daily life, it helps people create purpose from pain. Faith often provides language, rituals, and narratives that allow individuals to reframe their circumstances through a lens of hope and intentionality. And that same hope extends outward, shaping how we treat others. Many spiritual paths emphasize forgiveness, love, and a deep sense of communal care. In this way, our divine connection doesn't just transform our inner world—it spills over into our relationships.

Consider studies on regular prayer and meditation: participants consistently report lower stress, greater emotional well-being, and a more grounded sense of hope. These aren't just spiritual benefits—they're relational and physiological ones, too.

## The Role of Listening in Prayer and Meditation

When we think about prayer, it's easy to picture someone speaking—offering up words, pleas, praises. But what if true communication with the divine isn't just about talking? What if it's just as much about listening?

Many faith traditions across the world invite us into silence. Christian contemplative prayer, Buddhist mindfulness, and Sufi meditation all emphasize stillness—not as an escape from the world, but as a pathway to divine presence.

In that silence, we learn to notice, to interpret, to receive. Listening for God might mean sitting quietly with scripture, noticing signs in our daily lives, or simply acknowledging the inner nudge we feel deep in our gut.

Psalm 46:10 captures this well: "Be still, and know that I am God." Stillness isn't passive—it's an active kind of waiting. A trust that something sacred speaks when we slow down enough to hear it.


## Sacred Conversations Across Faith Traditions

Divine communication isn't a one-size-fits-all experience. Around the world, cultures and religions have developed their own ways of engaging in sacred conversation. In Christianity, for example, prayer can take many forms—petitionary (asking for help or guidance), intercessory (praying for others), or contemplative (simply being present with God in silence).

Across traditions, there's a shared belief that the divine speaks—not always audibly, but through scripture, inner conviction, community wisdom, or life events. Take Dr. Martin Luther King Jr., for instance. He often spoke of hearing God's call not in moments of comfort, but in the deepest valleys of doubt and struggle. It was this sense of divine conversation that fueled his courage to lead during one of the most turbulent times in American history.

## The Interplay of Self-Disclosure and Divine Connection

This leads us to an important idea: that communicating with the divine often reveals something about ourselves. The Johari Window model offers a helpful framework here. It teaches us that there are parts of our identity that we know and share, parts we keep hidden, parts others see that we don't, and parts that are completely unknown.

Spiritual practices like prayer, meditation, and journaling allow us to explore each of these layers.

We may bring our open selves—our joys, frustrations, hopes—into conversation with God. But in those moments, we might also find ourselves revealing what was hidden, or even discovering what was previously unknown. Sometimes, divine insight shows us a blind spot—a truth about ourselves we've overlooked. Other times, the process uncovers an identity or calling we didn't know we carried.

Divine communication can be a kind of self-disclosure that leads to transformation.

## Finding Meaning in Divine Communication

So, what's the takeaway in all of this? Communicating with the divine isn't just a spiritual checkbox. It's an ongoing conversation that can shape the way we see ourselves, relate to others, and navigate the world. Whether it comes through spoken prayer, silent meditation, sacred texts, or the quiet nudges of everyday life, divine communication invites us into something deeper.

It's not always about getting answers. More often, it's about building a relationship—anchoring ourselves in something bigger, wiser, and more loving than we can comprehend. In that space, we find connection. We grow. And we learn to trust, even when the path ahead isn't clear.

## *Chapter Three Reflection Questions*

1. When you strip away your roles, titles, and responsibilities, who are you at your core? What words would you use to describe your true self—the part of you that stays constant, even when everything else shifts?
2. How do you usually speak to yourself in moments of failure or insecurity? Would you use that same tone or language with someone you care about?
3. Have you ever been surprised by feedback from someone else? What did it reveal about how others see you—and how you see yourself?
4. Is there a part of your identity that you've outgrown, but still carry with you? Why do you think it's been hard to let go of that version of yourself?
5. What version of you are you becoming right now? Think about your current season of life. How is it shaping your self-perception?
6. Have you ever felt spiritually seen, guided, or spoken to in a quiet moment? What did that experience teach you about your identity or purpose?
7. What's one area of your "Blind Self" that you'd be open to exploring further? Who could you invite into that process with you?
8. In what ways has your self-talk shaped your confidence, decisions, or relationships this year? Where would you like to shift that inner dialogue?
9. What does it mean to you to "know yourself" spiritually, emotionally, and relationally? Is that something you feel you're growing in—or something you want to pursue more intentionally?
10. If you could tell your younger self one truth about who you are, what would you say? And just as importantly—what truth do you think your future self would want you to believe right now?

## *Chapter Three Challenges*

1. Practice Sacred Listening: Set aside 5–10 minutes this week to sit in silence. No music. No distractions.
   Ask: What is my soul trying to say that my brain keeps talking over? You don't have to "achieve" anything in this time. Just listen. You might be surprised at what surfaces.
2. Ask for Honest Feedback: Reach out to someone you trust and ask: "What's one strength you see in me that I might not fully recognize?"
   "What's one blind spot I should be aware of?"
   Sit with their answers. You don't have to agree with everything, but reflect on what resonates.
3. Write a Letter to Yourself: Write a short letter to the version of you from a year ago—or five years ago. Tell them what you've learned. Then write a letter from your future self to your current self. What encouragement would they give you? What truth would they want you to hold onto?
4. Speak Aloud a New Identity Statement: Say this out loud this week—maybe in the mirror, maybe before bed, maybe on a walk: "I am becoming someone who _____." Fill in the blank with a statement rooted in growth, truth, and possibility.

WE RELATE

# Chapter 4:

# How We Build Healthy Relationships

*"Happiness is not something ready-made. It comes from your own actions."*
— Dalai Lama

We spend a lot of time looking for the right people—swiping, scanning, hoping someone will walk into our lives and make it all make sense. But what if the most important relationship work doesn't start with who we meet—but with how we show up?

What if healthy connection isn't about finding someone to complete you, but becoming someone who is whole enough to connect well?

Not perfect, not polished. But emotionally grounded, relationally aware, and ready to build something real.

Think back to the last time you met someone new. Maybe it was in a class, at work, on an app, or in the cereal aisle. At first, there's a spark—energy, curiosity, potential. Conversations flow. Texts ping back and forth. You feel seen, maybe even a little high on the possibility.

But then something shifts. Maybe it deepens, or maybe it drifts. One day you're sharing inside jokes, the next you're rereading old texts wondering where it went.

So what happened?

That's the question we'll explore in this chapter—through science, stories, and reflection. We'll look at how relationships actually grow, what makes them last, and how your own habits, patterns, and emotional health play a much bigger role than you might think.

### The PERMA Model

Healthy relationships aren't built on chemistry alone. They're shaped by clarity, effort, and daily micro-decisions. And before we talk about "us," we need to start with *you*.

In the field of Positive Psychology, Dr. Martin Seligman's **PERMA model** outlines five core ingredients for a thriving, well-balanced life:

- **Positive Emotion** – joy, peace, hope, gratitude
- **Engagement** – deep focus, flow, presence
- **Relationships** – emotionally safe, mutual connection
- **Meaning** – purpose beyond yourself
- **Accomplishment** – progress, mastery, or growth

These aren't just wellness buzzwords. Think of them like nutrients for your emotional soil. When even one of these is chronically missing, connection becomes harder—not because you're broken, but because something in your foundation is off.

Maybe you've felt it. When you're burnt out, it's harder to be present with others. When you're unclear on your purpose, you might seek people to fill a void they were never meant to hold. When you don't feel seen or appreciated, even the happiest relationships can feel like a performance.

When these areas are balanced you become more grounded. You become more secure. You become more capable of building the kind of relationships that aren't just fun or flirty—but actually *fulfilling*.

**Think About It:** Which of the PERMA elements feels strong in your life right now? Which one feels undernourished? What small action could you take this week to nurture it?

### The External Arc: How Relationships Grow—and Sometimes Drift

Motivational speaker, life coach, and author Tony Robbins is known for saying that *"The quality of your life is the quality of your relationships."*

If our emotional foundation shapes how we show up, then what happens once we step into connection with someone else?

Relationships might feel spontaneous, like they "just happen"—a spark at a party, a mutual laugh in class, a slow burn from acquaintance to something more.

But underneath that surface magic, there's a structure. A rhythm. A pattern to how connections form, deepen, and sometimes fade.

## Relational Stages Model

Communication scholar Mark Knapp mapped this arc with his *Relational Stages Model*—a ten-stage journey that every relationship moves through in some way. Five stages bring people together. Five pull them apart. Think of it less like a checklist and more like a landscape: you don't always travel in order, and not every relationship visits every stop—but the terrain is familiar. Let's walk through it together.

## Phase 1: Coming Together

Every relationship starts with **Initiating**—first impressions and fast judgments. It's the smile across the room, the witty comment in a group chat, the "hey, I like your stickers" that sparks something small but real. You're scanning for signs: do I feel safe here? Curious? Intrigued?

Then comes **Experimenting**—the light conversation stage. Small talk, shared interests, finding common ground. It's the meme exchange, the "what are you watching?" texts, the "oh my god, you love that band too?" moment. The goal here isn't deep connection yet—it's potential. You're asking: is there something here to build on?

If there is, things move into **Intensifying**. Now, you're sharing more personal stories, texting late into the night, swapping secrets and Spotify playlists. You don't just like this person—you trust them. You're letting them see the real you. And you're starting to wonder what they might mean in your life.

In **Integrating**, your worlds start to merge. "Me" becomes "we." Others begin to think of you as a pair—friends, partners, a tight-knit team. Maybe you have shared rituals, or a favorite spot to hang out. Your identities get entangled—in ways that can feel incredibly affirming, but sometimes a little vulnerable, too.

Finally, there's **Bonding**—the public commitment phase. That might look like a Defining the Relationship (DTR) conversation, a best friend necklace, a social media announcement, or even moving in together. It's not just about closeness—it's about choosing to name it, honor it, and stand by it.

These early phases often feel exciting, full of potential. But what happens when things begin to shift?

## Phase 2: Coming Apart

Sometimes, the first signs of trouble are subtle. You enter **Differentiating**—where the focus shifts from similarities to differences. Suddenly, you're noticing the things that set you apart more than what brought you together. Maybe you want to slow down and they want to speed up. Maybe your values start to clash. Maybe you just feel... off.

If this distance goes unspoken, you might move into **Circumscribing**—where communication becomes shallow. The real stuff feels too loaded, too risky. You stop asking real questions. You stick to safe topics. Conversations shrink to logistics and surface-level check-ins.

Eventually, you may hit **Stagnating**—where things feel stuck. The emotional energy is gone. You're going through the motions, saying the same things, replaying the same conversations. You're still technically "connected," but you feel more like strangers than soulmates.

Then comes **Avoiding**—intentional distance. You cancel plans, let texts pile up, or start feeling relief when they don't reach out. It's not just busyness—it's withdrawal. The desire to protect yourself from awkwardness, resentment, or the ache of a fading bond.

Finally, there's **Terminating**. Sometimes it's dramatic: a falling-out, a breakup, a "we're done" moment. Other times, it's a quiet fade. A relationship that used to be everything becomes just a memory.

## Fast-Forwarded Feelings: Pop Culture in Real Time

You can actually see all of these stages in action—in just ten days—in the chaotic romantic comedy *How to Lose a Guy in 10 Days*.

At first, Andy and Ben are both pretending—each with hidden motives. But as they move from flirtation to frustration to actual affection, they cycle through every stage: initiating, experimenting, intensifying, differentiating, avoiding. And yet, even in the absurdity, there's something real.

In real relationships, we do this too: we perform. We protect. We try. We pull away. We show our cards too soon or not at all.

The arc of their fictional relationship reminds us that even the most outrageous setups can reflect something deeply human: we all want to be seen and chosen—not just for the version of ourselves we perform, but for the one we actually are.

## Two Friendships, Two Outcomes

Sarah's story echoes this truth in a different way. In her first year of college, she watched two friendships take radically different paths. One faded, quietly, after high school graduation—no falling out, just a slow drift. The other, against the odds, grew stronger, even with distance. They made time. They stayed curious. They eventually fell in love and started a family.

The difference wasn't proximity, it wasn't fate. It was effort.

That story shows us what Knapp's Relational Development model can't fully capture: that relationships aren't linear—they're *lived*. And the choices we make inside them—whether to reach out or retreat, to ask the hard question or stay silent—shape everything.

**Think About It:** Consider a current relationship in your life. Where do you see yourself in the relational arc right now? What's one small step you could take to move it forward—or honor where it's naturally landing?

## Why We React the Way We Do:
### Nervous Systems and Attachment Styles

Have you ever told yourself you didn't care about someone's delayed reply, only to find yourself checking your phone ten times in five minutes? Or felt the need to withdraw from someone you genuinely care about, even when you were longing for connection? These reactions might seem confusing, but they're not irrational—they're deeply wired responses from your nervous system.

Relationships affect more than just our emotions. They shape our physiology. Every interaction—whether it's a warm hug, an unresolved silence, or a message left on read—triggers a biological response. Understanding how your body processes connection, stress, and vulnerability can change the way you interpret your patterns—and help you build better ones.

Let's start with three key players in the chemistry of connection: oxytocin, cortisol, and dopamine.

Oxytocin, often called the "bonding hormone," is released when we feel emotionally safe and physically close. This happens during long hugs, eye contact, or deep, attentive conversations. It's what gives us that grounded, settled feeling when we're around people we trust. Oxytocin calms the nervous system and builds a sense of security.

But when a relationship feels unpredictable, emotionally distant, or unsafe, the body releases cortisol—its primary stress hormone. Cortisol is designed to help us survive emergencies, but when we're flooded with it consistently—like when we're constantly guessing where we stand with someone—it wears us down. We may feel irritable, anxious, or physically depleted.

Dopamine, meanwhile, fuels excitement. It spikes when we receive validation or experience novelty. That thrill when someone texts you back or likes your post? That's dopamine. It's also the chemical that keeps us chasing attention, even in relationships that leave us feeling unsteady. The more unpredictable the reward, the more addictive it becomes.

One student once told me she felt addicted to her situationship. "I was either on a high or spiraling," she said. "I couldn't sleep. I couldn't focus. I kept telling myself I didn't care, but my body told a different story." Her experience wasn't about willpower—it was a nervous system trying to navigate uncertainty and craving connection.

### Attachment Theory: Different Styles of Relating
This is where attachment theory comes in. If your nervous system is the hardware, your attachment style is the software—it's the emotional script you've developed based on early relationships and experiences.

Attachment theory, first developed by John Bowlby and Mary Ainsworth, explains how we tend to relate to others emotionally. There are four main attachment styles, each reflecting different ways of navigating closeness, conflict, and vulnerability.

People with a **secure attachment** style feel comfortable with both intimacy and independence. They can ask for what they need, offer support in return, and believe that relationships can be repaired when they hit rough patches.

Those with an **anxious attachment** style often crave closeness but fear rejection. They might overanalyze texts, seek reassurance frequently, or feel like they're "too much" for others.

An **avoidant attachment** style shows up as a discomfort with emotional closeness. These individuals often pride themselves on self-reliance and may pull away when things get too vulnerable.

Then there's the **disorganized attachment** style—a mix of both anxious and avoidant tendencies. These individuals often desire connection deeply, but also fear it, leading to confusing or contradictory behaviors.

One student explained her experience this way: "When people get close, I push them away. But when they leave, I panic." Her behavior wasn't random—it was patterned, shaped by past experiences of instability and loss. Once she learned to recognize that pattern, she could approach her reactions with more clarity and compassion, rather than shame.

The important thing to know about attachment styles is that they aren't fixed. They're not diagnoses. They're starting points—adaptations we've built to stay emotionally safe. And with awareness, practice, and intentional relationships, we can move closer to secure.

**Think About It:** When a relationship feels strained, do you tend to pull away, seek closeness, shut down, or try to resolve things? What does that tell you about how you've learned to protect yourself in connection? Can you trace these patterns back to earlier experiences? And more importantly, are they still serving you now?

## Navigating the Push and Pull

Even the healthiest relationships are full of contradictions. You want to feel close, but you also need space. You crave consistency, but you don't want things to get boring. You long to be truly known, but you also want to keep certain parts of yourself private. These aren't necessarily signs that something's wrong; they may be indicators that something's real.

Communication scholars Leslie Baxter and Barbara Montgomery call this the **Relational Dialectics Theory**—the idea that relationships are not static, but ongoing negotiations between competing desires.

Every close relationship, whether it's a friendship, romance, or family bond, is shaped by these tensions. They don't mean you're incompatible. They mean you're human.

There are three especially common dialectical tensions that show up again and again:

First is **connection versus independence**. We want to feel bonded to others, to know someone has our back. But we also need room to breathe, to grow, to retain a sense of self. Too much togetherness can start to feel smothering. Too much independence can feel like abandonment.

Next is **predictability versus novelty**. Comfort comes from routine—inside jokes, shared habits, familiar rituals. But too much routine can feel stale. Relationships need some level of unpredictability, surprise, or growth to stay alive. The healthiest connections often dance between these two—finding safety in rhythm, but also making room for reinvention.

And then there's **openness versus privacy**. Vulnerability builds intimacy, but it also exposes us. In strong relationships, we share thoughts, fears, and truths—but that doesn't mean everything is (or should be) on the table all the time. Boundaries matter. Privacy matters. The key is not total openness, but intentional openness—knowing when and how to share in a way that deepens trust.

You've likely felt these tensions in your own life. Maybe you've been in a friendship where one person wanted constant closeness, while the other needed more space. Or in a relationship that started off exciting, then began to feel stuck in routine. Or maybe you've held back from sharing something important—not because you didn't care, but because you weren't sure how it would be received.

These aren't problems to be fixed. They're dynamics to be navigated. The goal isn't to eliminate tension, but to become more fluent in it—more able to talk about needs before they turn into resentment.

We see this clearly illustrated in pop culture, like in *The Office*, where Jim and Pam's relationship—rooted in deep connection—hits a turning point when Jim takes a job in another city. Pam wrestles with her desire for stability and her support for Jim's growth. It's not about one of them being wrong—it's about finding new rhythms for an evolving relationship.

But navigating these tensions isn't just about internal balance. It's also about fairness.

That's where **Equity Theory** comes in—a concept that highlights the importance of reciprocity in relationships. Developed by psychologist J. Stacy Adams, the theory suggests that people feel most satisfied in relationships where the give-and-take feels mutual—not necessarily equal, but balanced.

Equity doesn't mean splitting everything 50/50. Some seasons are unbalanced on purpose—when one person is grieving, burned out, or in transition. But over time, the relationship needs to feel like both people are contributing in meaningful ways.

When one person is always initiating, listening, planning, or giving—and the other is consistently on the receiving end—something starts to shift.

Sometimes, the imbalance is subtle: a friend who always needs advice but rarely asks how you're doing. A partner who depends on your emotional labor but isn't emotionally available themselves.

At first, you may not notice. Maybe you're naturally generous, or conflict-avoidant, or just hopeful. But over time, something starts to ache. You feel invisible, or depleted, or quietly resentful.

This emotional math—this sense of the relationship not "adding up"—can lead to what researchers call **relational drift**. It's not always dramatic. It's a slow erosion, a sense that the connection isn't what it used to be—and maybe never was.

A vivid example of this comes from *Insecure*, where Issa and Molly's friendship begins as a model of support and closeness. But over time, unspoken frustrations build. Their lives begin to diverge, and both women start to feel like they're giving more than they're receiving. The relationship doesn't rupture from a single argument—it frays through avoidance, unmet expectations, and emotional imbalance. What was once mutual becomes lopsided. What was once effortless begins to feel heavy.

And it's not just about effort—it's also about emotional presence. Showing up, not just physically, but attentively. Feeling heard, feeling known, feeling like your care is being returned.

**Think About It:** Where have you felt a tension between closeness and space—or between routine and change—in a relationship that mattered to you? Have you ever felt like you were carrying the weight of a relationship on your own? What conversations might have helped restore balance or clarify expectations?

**Habits That Strengthen Connection**
Understanding relationships is important—but what truly builds and sustains them are the habits we bring into them every day. Not grand gestures or dramatic breakthroughs, but small, consistent actions that say: *I'm here. I care. I'm willing to show up.*

These habits shape the emotional climate of a relationship. They determine whether someone feels safe with you, whether you feel seen in return, and whether both of you have the space to be fully human—messy, changing, learning, and growing.

One of the most foundational habits is simple—but not always easy: **naming what you need**. A lot of tension in relationships comes from unspoken expectations. We assume people should "just know" what we're thinking or feeling. When they don't, we internalize disappointment or lash out in frustration.

But no one can read your mind. And connection deepens when you communicate needs with clarity, not blame. Instead of saying, "You never text me back," try, "Hey, I've been feeling a little disconnected lately—can we check in more regularly?" It's honest. It's specific. And it invites understanding instead of defensiveness.

Another essential habit is **repairing after conflict**. No matter how strong a relationship is, ruptures will happen—miscommunications, missed cues, moments when emotions run high. The difference between relationships that grow and relationships that fracture is what happens *next*.

Repair doesn't require a perfect apology. Sometimes it's a short message that says, "I overreacted. Can we talk?" or "That didn't come out the way I meant it—I'm sorry." These moments of vulnerability, especially when they're genuine and timely, build more trust than any conflict could break.

Boundaries are another key piece of relational health—but they're often misunderstood. A boundary isn't a punishment or a wall. It's a door with a handle. It's saying, "Here's what I need in order to stay grounded and present in this relationship."

That might mean asking for time alone to recharge. Saying no to emotional labor that leaves you depleted. Or clarifying your availability instead of ghosting or avoiding.

Boundaries don't push people away—they create the conditions for sustainable closeness.

**Presence** is perhaps the most underrated relationship skill of all. In a world that constantly pulls our attention in a dozen directions, offering someone your full focus is a gift. You don't need the perfect advice. Just listen. Ask real questions. Be curious about their answers. Instead of "How was your day?" try "When did you feel most alive today?" The shift is subtle—but powerful.

Relational health isn't about getting everything right. It's about being willing to *practice*. To keep showing up. To notice when something feels off, and rather than ignoring it or overcompensating, choosing to get curious and move with intention.

**Think About It:** What are the relationship habits you rely on most? Which ones come naturally to you—gratitude, communication, emotional presence? Which ones do you avoid? And what's one small shift you could try to strengthen a connection that matters to you?

## Evaluating Your Relationships

You probably keep an eye on your grades, your finances, maybe even your physical health. But how often do you pause to evaluate your relationships—not just how many you have, but how they're functioning?

Think of your relationships like a **portfolio** of investments. A wise investor doesn't put everything into one stock—they diversify. They pay attention to risk, return, and value over time. Healthy relational lives work the same way. You need a mix of connection types—some that are deep and grounding, others that are energizing and lighthearted. You also need to know where you're overextending—and where you might be underinvesting in the connections that truly matter.

Your relational portfolio might include:
- Close friends you confide in
- Romantic partners or situationships
- Roommates, classmates, or coworkers
- Mentors, coaches, or teachers
- Family or chosen family
- People who've walked with you through crisis or transformation
- Communities—spiritual, creative, activist, or cultural

Not every person needs to be everything to you—and they shouldn't be. A healthy ecosystem of connection includes variety.

What matters most is that the relationships you're investing in offer something real in return: emotional safety, mutual support, shared growth, joy, honesty, or presence.

One student shared that most of her relational energy was going to two places: her long-distance boyfriend and her coworkers. Between managing the demands of both, she had unintentionally let go of the friendships that had sustained her through some of her hardest seasons. "I didn't even realize I was relationally overleveraged," she said. "I was surviving my social life instead of building something that could hold me."

That's the risk we face when we stop reviewing our relationships. We can end up pouring time and energy into people out of obligation, attraction, or habit—while neglecting the relationships that actually nourish us.

This isn't about blame. It's about noticing. Because attention is a form of care, and how you spend your relational energy shapes how you experience your life.

Taking stock helps you see more clearly—not just who's in your life, but how each relationship functions. Some connections stretch you. Some steady you. Some leave you feeling unseen, exhausted, or quietly diminished.

You don't need to cut everyone out to restore balance. Sometimes, a simple shift—reaching out, setting a boundary, asking a better question—can reshape the dynamic.

**Think About It:** Where are you currently investing most of your relational energy? Are you pouring into people who can't—or won't—offer anything in return? Are there steady, grounding relationships you've been unintentionally neglecting? What would it look like to realign your portfolio so it actually supports your growth?

## Bringing It All Together

Relational health isn't something you're born with or something you figure out once and for all. It's something you *build*. Over time. Through reflection, through practice, through moments of courage and care. It's something you create through the choices you make each day—who you show up for, how you communicate, and whether you're willing to be honest about what you need.

By now, you've explored a lot. You've seen how connection begins—how it moves from first impressions to deepening intimacy, and how it can drift or dissolve when care goes missing. You've considered how your nervous system and early experiences shape your reactions to closeness, conflict, or change.

You've also learned that even the healthiest relationships carry tension, and that what matters isn't eliminating that tension, but learning to navigate it with presence and respect.

You've looked closely at the habits that build safety—like repair, boundary-setting, naming your needs, and listening without fixing. And maybe most importantly, you've taken time to reflect on your relational portfolio—the people, patterns, and investments that make up the emotional architecture of your life.

And here's the thread that connects it all: *you have agency*. You're not stuck. You're not at the mercy of who does or doesn't text back, who stays, or who fades. You have the ability to influence your relational world—not through control, but through clarity. Through the way you show up. Through the way you choose to respond, to repair, to realign.

That doesn't mean forcing every relationship to last. Some connections are meant for a season, and letting them go can be a healthy, even healing choice. But it *does* mean paying attention to what you're creating moment by moment, word by word, habit by habit.

It's not about perfection. It's about alignment. Intention. Practice.

**Think About It:** What kind of relationships are you trying to build—not just in theory, but in practice? What do you want connection to feel like in your life: safe, reciprocal, real? What's one small habit you can begin or return to this week to help bring that vision closer to reality?

Healthy relationships aren't built overnight. But every honest conversation, every thoughtful check-in, every effort to listen, repair, or speak up—these are the building blocks. They may feel small in the moment. But over time, they shape the emotional landscape you live in.

And that landscape matters. You live there every day.

So choose wisely. Show up honestly. Keep building something that lasts not just in others, but in yourself.

## *Chapter Four Reflection Questions*

1. In your relationships, do you tend to take the lead in emotional labor (initiating, checking in, repairing), or do you tend to wait for the other person to act? How does that dynamic impact your sense of connection?
2. Looking at your relational "portfolio," which relationships feel nourishing and reciprocal—and which ones feel draining or one-sided? What might need to shift?
3. Consider a relationship that recently changed—deepened, drifted, or ended. Can you trace which stage of the relational arc it was in? What decisions or patterns moved it that direction?
4. When conflict arises, what's your default response—shutting down, fixing, withdrawing, clinging, avoiding? Where do you think that response comes from?
5. Which relational dialectic (connection vs. independence, predictability vs. novelty, openness vs. privacy) shows up most often for you? How do you typically navigate it?
6. What does fairness in a relationship mean to you? How do you notice when a relationship feels out of balance?
7. What habits do you bring into relationships that strengthen connection? Which habits might be unintentionally creating distance or confusion?
8. What is your current attachment style, and how has it shaped your experiences of closeness or vulnerability? What are you learning about how to move toward secure connection?
9. When do you feel most emotionally safe with someone? What do they do—or not do—that helps you feel seen and respected?

## *Chapter Four Challenges*

1. The 48-Hour Relational Reset. Choose one relationship in your life and make an intentional communication shift for the next two days. That could mean initiating a real check-in, practicing active listening, expressing appreciation, or setting a needed boundary. Notice what shifts in tone, energy, or connection.
2. The Portfolio Review. Sketch out your current relational ecosystem. Who are your primary connections? Label them: Nourishing, Neutral, or Draining. Then identify one underinvested relationship you'd like to nurture—and one overextended one you may need to reevaluate.
3. Name a Need. Practice clear, non-defensive communication by expressing one emotional need in a relationship where you often stay quiet. Keep it direct, kind, and focused on clarity—not blame. For example: "I've been feeling distant lately—could we plan some intentional time together soon?"
4. Attachment Awareness Moment. The next time you feel anxious, distant, or unsure in a relationship, pause and notice your pattern. Are you reacting from an old script? Try responding in a way that aligns with the secure connection you're trying to build.
5. Daily Habit Tracker. For five days, track one healthy relational habit—such as offering appreciation, listening without interrupting, or resisting the urge to overfunction. Each day, jot a quick note about what happened and how it felt to show up differently.

# WE RELATE

# Chapter 5:

# Relationships and Communication

*"The single biggest problem in communication is the illusion that it has taken place."*
— *George Bernard Shaw*

### Why Is Communication the Foundation of Every Relationship?

Have you ever walked away from a conversation thinking, *Well, that went well,* only to find out later that the other person was offended, confused, or upset? Or maybe you've sent a simple "Okay." text, only to have the recipient ask, "Are you mad at me?"

The truth is, most of us assume we're better communicators than we actually are. We think we're being clear, but words get twisted, tone gets misread, and nonverbal cues—like eye rolls, crossed arms, or a hesitant pause—speak volumes we don't always hear.

Communication is the foundation of every relationship, but it's also one of the biggest sources of conflict.

This chapter unpacks why communication breaks down, how nonverbal cues shape our interactions, and what separates strong communicators from those who constantly feel misunderstood. Get ready to rethink how you express yourself and how well you truly listen.

The way we communicate can either strengthen or weaken our relationships. From verbal exchanges to subtle nonverbal cues, effective communication is more than just saying words—it's about ensuring the message is truly received.

**Pop Culture: Ross & Rachel—'We Were on a Break'**
One of the most debated moments in pop culture history comes from *Friends*, when Ross and Rachel's relationship implodes over the infamous *"We were on a break"* misunderstanding. Ross assumes the break means they're free to see other people; Rachel doesn't. The lack of clear communication leads to heartbreak, drama, and years of emotional baggage.

**The Inspiring Story of *Malala Yousafzai***
Communication isn't just about personal relationships—it's the key to changing the world. Malala Yousafzai was just 11 when she started speaking out for girls' education in Pakistan, using the power of words to challenge the Taliban's restrictions.

Despite surviving an assassination attempt, she continued her advocacy, proving that words can be more powerful than weapons. Her journey reminds us that communication isn't just about what we say—it's about how we use our voice to inspire action.

## A Lesson in Active Listening

As professors, we see students' real struggles with communication every day—whether it's a disagreement with a roommate or misreading a professor's feedback. For example, Trey's student once shared how she felt unheard in a group project. When he asked her if she had clearly expressed her concerns, she realized she had assumed the others understood her frustration without explicitly saying it. It was a classic case of expecting people to read minds—a mistake we all make in relationships.

**Think About It:** When have you miscommunicated with someone. What caused the misunderstanding? Chances are, it wasn't just the words you used—or didn't use.

Often, miscommunication happens in the spaces between our sentences: the raised eyebrow, the rushed tone, the long pause that goes unspoken. We assume others "get it" because we feel something strongly, but unless we match our emotions with clear words and cues, people are left guessing. This brings us to one of the most overlooked truths in human connection:

## Verbal vs. Nonverbal: More Than Just Words

Studies show that as little as 7% of communication is verbal, or the words we use; the rest is our tone (38%) and body language (55%) (Mehrabian, 1971). That means our gestures, facial expressions, and even the way we pause can shape the meaning of our words. Consider how a simple "I'm fine" can mean wildly different things depending on tone and body language.

## Active Listening: Are You Really Hearing Them?

Many people listen to respond rather than to understand. Active listening is the practice of fully focusing on the speaker, avoiding interruptions, and reflecting back what they said to ensure clarity.

## Improve Your Active Listening

One of the most powerful tools you can bring into any relationship is the ability to *truly listen*. More than hearing words, making the other person feel genuinely heard. That type of listening is rare—and it sets strong communicators apart. It starts with giving your full attention.

That means maintaining eye contact, putting down your phone, and mentally showing up. No multitasking, no nodding while scrolling through emails. When someone is sharing something meaningful—whether it's a stressful day or a big dream—being fully present tells them, *"You matter right now."*

Once they've spoken, try reflecting back what you heard with a phrase like, *"So what I hear you saying is…"* It might feel awkward at first, but it helps confirm you've understood—not just the facts, but the feeling behind the words. And if something isn't clear? Ask a question. Not a leading or defensive one, but a curious, open-ended one. It shows you care enough not to assume.

Of course, in today's world, much of our communication doesn't happen face-to-face—it happens through screens. Texting and social media make it incredibly easy to stay connected across time zones, friend groups, and life stages. But digital communication also comes with a cost. Tone can be hard to read in a text message. A short reply like "Okay." can come across as passive-aggressive or dismissive, even if it was meant as totally neutral.

Without facial expressions or vocal tone, it's easy to misinterpret someone's intent. Then there's the issue of timing. Digital communication allows for delayed responses—or no response at all. Ghosting, once reserved for awkward first dates, can now happen in friendships, work conversations, and even family group chats.

That delay—or complete silence—can stir up anxiety, confusion, or self-doubt. And let's not forget the performance pressure of social media. Platforms like Instagram and TikTok encourage people to curate and share only the best parts of their lives.

That curated reality can skew our expectations and lead us to compare our everyday mess to someone else's highlight reel, affecting how we relate and communicate with others.

## Conflict Resolution Styles

So what happens when communication breaks down or disagreements arise? Enter the five classic conflict resolution styles, based on the Thomas-Kilmann model. Each of us tends to lean toward one or more of these when tensions rise.

The *Avoiding* style is just what it sounds like—dodging the issue, changing the subject, or disappearing altogether. *Competing* is the opposite: going in to win, regardless of the emotional cost. Then there's *Accommodating*, where one person yields or gives in to keep the peace.

This can work short-term but often builds resentment if it becomes a pattern. *Compromising* means both sides give up a little to meet in the middle—it's fair, but it may not fully satisfy either party. Finally, *Collaborating* is the ideal (though often the hardest): it's when both people engage fully, share perspectives, and work toward a win-win solution.

Imagine a workplace disagreement: the avoider ignores the tension, the competitor insists on their idea, but the collaborator says, "Let's sit down and figure out something that works for both of us." That's the kind of approach that builds lasting trust.

**The Gottman Ratio: Predicting the Success of Love**
Relationship researchers have found that it's not just how we handle conflict, but how we balance it that matters. According to Dr. John Gottman, one of the leading experts on marital communication, the most stable and successful relationships maintain a 5:1 ratio.

The **5:1 Ratio** states that for every negative interaction, a couple must have at least five positive ones to maintain happiness. It's not about never arguing, but about balancing out the tension with moments of care. A couple might bicker about chores, but if that's followed by a kind gesture, shared laugh, or quick hug, the connection remains strong.

That same principle applies to friendships, teams, and families. When criticism or conflict shows up, what matters is how much positive reinforcement is also present to anchor the relationship in trust and warmth.

Lastly, it's essential to remember that communication isn't universal. It's deeply shaped by culture and gender, and what counts as "effective" or "clear" communication can vary widely. In some cultures—like the U.S., Germany, or the Netherlands—direct communication is expected and valued. People say what they mean, and clarity is considered respectful.

In other cultures—like Japan, India, or Mexico—indirect communication is more common. People may use nonverbal cues, silence, or suggestion to convey meaning, especially in emotionally sensitive situations. Even within the same culture, gender can influence how people communicate.

Research shows that men often listen for solutions and may interrupt more during debates, while women tend to listen for empathy and connection. This doesn't mean one style is better—it just means differences can lead to misunderstandings if we're not aware of them. Eye contact, physical space, tone, and gesture all vary across cultures too. A direct gaze might be seen as confidence in one culture, and disrespect in another.

So when communicating across lines of culture, gender, or background, empathy and curiosity are your best tools. Ask, observe, and don't assume.

## Who Holds the Power in a Conversation?

Have you ever sat in a meeting and watched someone get cut off—over and over—while someone else seems to command the room without even trying? Or maybe you've made a point, only to watch it get noticed when someone else repeats it? That's not coincidence. That's power showing up in real time.

Power dynamics don't just live in titles or résumés. They show up in eye contact, speaking time, interruptions, and whose voices get validated. And often, we're not even aware it's happening.

**Howard Giles' Communication Accommodation Theory (CAT)** offers insight here. It suggests that people instinctively adjust their speech to match the perceived power or social status of the person they're speaking to. For instance, a new employee might speak more formally in front of leadership but slip into slang with coworkers.

Meanwhile, someone in power may not adjust at all—sending the subtle message that their voice is the standard others must match. This plays out in larger patterns, too. A foundational study by Zimmerman & West (1975) found that men interrupt women significantly more often in professional settings. Decades later, research continues to show that marginalized voices—women, people of color, LGBTQIA+ individuals—are more likely to be interrupted, ignored, or dismissed, even when they hold expertise.

So what do we do about it? If you're in a position of power—whether by title, identity, or experience—use your voice to create space for others. When you see someone being cut off, say, *"Let's hear them finish."* If you notice someone hasn't spoken yet, ask, *"Would you like to weigh in?"* Power used with intention becomes inclusion.

If you often feel unheard, you can start practicing strategic assertiveness. That might sound like: *"As I was saying earlier, I think this connects back to..."* or *"I'd love to finish my thought before we move on."* You don't have to yell to take up space— you just have to stand in it.

**Think About It:** Have you ever noticed subtle power dynamics in your conversations? When do you feel heard—and when do you shrink back? What roles do you tend to play in group settings?

## Expectancy Violations Theory

Imagine expecting a warm hug but receiving a handshake . Or sending a long, heartfelt message only to get a "K." in response. Expectancy Violations Theory (EVT; Burgoon, 1978) explains how people react when their expectations of communication behavior are disrupted.

Violations can be positive (an unexpected compliment) or negative (being ignored in a conversation). The interpretation depends on who is violating the expectation—a surprise visit from a close friend may feel welcome, while from an acquaintance, it could feel intrusive.

Digital communication has created new norms and new violations—delayed responses, short texts, and leaving someone on "read" can create unintended tension. Recognizing that expectations vary across individuals and contexts helps us navigate miscommunication with patience and understanding.

**The Rise of Social Media Anxiety**
While social media can help us stay connected, research shows that it can also increase anxiety and loneliness. The "highlight reel effect"—where people present only the most curated, polished versions of their lives—can lead to unrealistic comparisons and feelings of inadequacy (Twenge et al., 2018).

To combat this, experts suggest setting boundaries for online interactions, engaging in digital detoxes, and prioritizing face-to-face communication to maintain healthy relationships.

**Why is "No" So Hard to Say?**
We've all been there—someone asks for a favor, and even though we're exhausted, we say yes anyway. Or we keep texting that one friend who only reaches out when they need something, even though we know it's draining.

This is where **Relational Dialectics Theory** (Baxter & Montgomery, 1996) comes in. Every relationship is a balancing act between connection and autonomy. As we will explore in a later chapter, setting boundaries—knowing when to say no—isn't about shutting people out. It's about preserving energy for the relationships that matter most.

Many people fear saying "no" because they don't want to disappoint others. But in healthy relationships, setting boundaries is an act of self-respect, not selfishness.

Research shows that people who struggle with boundary-setting report higher stress, anxiety, and burnout (Brown, 2010). Saying no isn't selfish—it's an act of self-care.

Instead of overexplaining when setting a boundary (*"I wish I could, but I have so much going on, and maybe later?"*), try simple phrases like, *"I appreciate the invite, but I need some time to recharge."* Or, *"I can't commit to that project right now, but I'd love to help in a smaller way."*

**Think About It:** When was the last time you said yes when you wanted to say no? How did it make you feel?

### Neurodiversity and Communication Styles

Not everyone communicates the same way. Neurodivergent individuals—such as those with autism, ADHD, or dyslexia process social cues, verbal exchanges, and body language differently than neurotypical individuals.

For example, autistic individuals may prefer direct, literal communication, while neurotypicals rely heavily on implied meaning and nonverbal cues (Brown & Klein, 2020).

Understanding neurodivergent perspectives fosters more inclusive and respectful conversations, whether in friendships, romantic relationships, or workplaces.

Instead of assuming someone's communication style is "wrong" or "awkward," consider adapting and being open to different ways of expressing thoughts and emotions.

## It All Comes Back to Communication

At the core of every meaningful relationship is one constant: communication. Not just the words we speak, but the way we show up—through eye contact, through pauses, through body language, through the choice to listen instead of responding right away.

Communication is the current that carries every emotion, every misunderstanding, every spark of connection between people. It's how we build trust, how we repair damage, and how we feel known.

Throughout this chapter, we've explored how relationships evolve—how they are shaped by stages, tensions, and the sense of balance or imbalance we feel. We've looked at what happens when connection is strong and what it feels like when it begins to slip.

We've talked about the quiet power of listening, the complexity of digital conversations, and the ways culture and conflict influence how we relate. And at every point, the theme is the same: communication is the tool we use to either build bridges or burn them.

You don't have to be an expert to be a better communicator. You just have to be curious. Curious about how your words land. Curious about what someone else is feeling beneath what they're saying. Curious about your own patterns—what you avoid, what you rush, what you over-explain.

Small shifts matter. The choice to ask for clarity. The choice to check your assumptions. The choice to slow down instead of snapping. These are acts of care, and they create space for deeper relationships.

The truth is, connection doesn't usually fall apart because people don't care. It falls apart because we don't know how to express it. When we learn to communicate with empathy, honesty, and intentionality, everything changes.

## *Chapter Five Reflection Questions*

1. What's one relationship in your life where communication feels easy and natural? What do you think makes that possible?
2. What's one relationship where communication feels hard, tense, or awkward? What do you think contributes to that dynamic?
3. When someone disagrees with you, how do you typically respond—defensively, curiously, passively, or something else? Why?
4. How do you feel when someone interrupts you or seems distracted while you're talking? Do you ever catch yourself doing the same to others?
5. Ever said something you didn't mean—via text, email, or face-to-face—that was misinterpreted and caused harm? What did you learn from that moment?
6. When conflict arises, do you try to resolve it quickly, avoid it, or go silent? Where do you think that instinct comes from—family, culture, past experiences?
7. What's one assumption you've made recently that turned out to be wrong? How could clearer communication have changed the outcome?
8. What role does humor play in your communication style? Do you use it to connect, deflect, or cope?
9. Think about your digital communication habits. How often do you reread texts before sending? How often do you read into punctuation, tone, or delay?
10. Who in your life makes you feel truly listened to? What do they do that makes their listening feel different—and how can you adopt those habits?

## *Chapter Five Challenges*

1. Mirror Challenge. Pick one person in your life and, for one full day, mirror their communication style—not to mimic, but to understand. If they're soft-spoken, try slowing your voice. If they use expressive gestures, engage with more body language. Take mental notes: *How does their style shape the way others respond to them? What does it feel like to communicate differently?*
2. The "One Thing You Never Say" Challenge. This week, choose one positive thought you often think but rarely say aloud—like "I admire how she handles stress" or "He makes people feel safe." Find the moment and say it. You might be surprised how powerful it is to speak what's usually kept inside.
3. The Five-Minute Face-to-Face. Schedule five intentional minutes with someone you usually only text. No distractions, no small talk—just ask one meaningful question and stay fully present. (Examples: "What's been on your mind lately?" or "What's something you wish people asked you more often?")
4. The Nonverbal Reset. Spend one full conversation being radically aware of your body language. What are your arms doing? Are you nodding, tilting your head, furrowing your brow? Then switch it up: lean in, soften your face, open your posture. Notice how it shifts the tone of the exchange.
5. The Pause & Paraphrase Practice. In your next disagreement or emotionally charged moment, pause before responding. Then try to paraphrase the other person's message *before* making your point. ("So it sounds like you're feeling left out because I didn't loop you in—is that right?") See how that affects the outcome.

# PART 2:

# THE WAY WE RELATE

**Relationships Have Changed Over Time**
From family bonds that shape our very identities to friendships, romantic relationships, and mentorships that stretch across decades, this part of the book dives into the ways our personal and professional connections differ from each other, how they shift over time, and what we can do to nurture them.

Think back to your childhood best friend—the one you spent endless afternoons with, whispering secrets and making grand plans. Now compare that to your relationships with your friendships now. Are they just as carefree? Or have they evolved and been shaped by time, distance, and experience?

Relationships evolve as we move through different life stages. Childhood friendships are based on proximity and shared play, young adult relationships focus on identity and emotional intimacy, and adult relationships require effort to maintain as life responsibilities increase.

Research suggests that people in their 40s and 50s prioritize a few deep connections over large social circles, while older adults often focus on legacy and emotional closeness (Carstensen et al., 2003). Understanding these different types of relationships can help us appreciate their unique qualities at different seasons of life.

## *What We'll Explore in This Section:*

Part 2 takes a deep dive into the different types of relationships that define our lives, from family ties to friendships to romantic partnerships to workplace relationships. Understanding how these relationships change helps us navigate them with greater intention and grace.

## Chapter 6: Family and Intergenerational Communication

Our families shape us in profound ways, influencing how we see the world and interact with others. But family relationships aren't always easy.

This chapter explores birth order, parenting styles, and the challenges of intergenerational communication, including how to break unhealthy patterns and build stronger family bonds.

## Chapter 7: Friendship in the Modern World

Friendships are some of the most defining relationships in our lives, yet they don't come with a clear set of rules.

We will explore how friendships evolve from childhood to adulthood, the impact of digital communication on social bonds, and the bittersweet reality of letting go when a friendship no longer serves us.

## Chapter 8: The Dynamics of Romantic Relationships

Romantic relationships are complex, exhilarating, and sometimes challenging. What makes some love stories last while others fade? This chapter unpacks the science of attraction, attachment styles, and the key ingredients of lasting relationships, from communication to trust to shared values.

## Chapter 9: Communication in the Workplace – Building Meaningful Professional Relationships

Our professional relationships can have a profound impact on not only the trajectory of our careers but our overall wellbeing. This chapter discusses how effective workplace communication can contribute to our sense of professional purpose and connection.

## The Core Idea: Relationships Require Adaptability

A major truth about relationships is that they are not static—they change, and so must we.

The friendships, family ties, and romantic relationships that serve us at one point in life may look very different years down the road. But the key to lasting, meaningful relationships is learning how to adapt, communicate, and prioritize the connections that truly matter.

By the end of this section, you'll have a deeper understanding of how different relationships evolve, why some last and others don't, and what we can do to nurture strong, fulfilling connections throughout our lives.

Let's explore the journey of human relationships and how they grow, shift, and endure.

# WE RELATE

# Chapter 6:

# Family and Intergenerational Communication

*"Family is not an important thing, it's everything."*
*— Michael J. Fox*

**How Do Family Dynamics Shape Us?**
Our family relationships are the first and often most influential connections we experience. From the way we communicate with parents and siblings to the deep-rooted values passed down through generations, family shapes our worldview, communication style, and even our relationships outside the home.

But family is not always simple—sometimes, we must break cycles, set boundaries, and learn how to bridge generational gaps to foster healthier connections.

In this chapter, we examine how birth order, family culture, and parenting styles influence us, the challenges of healing from toxic family dynamics, and practical ways to communicate effectively across generations.

*Family Influences in Action*
The psychological theory that birth order impacts personality and communication is often debated, but pop culture provides some striking examples. In *Succession*, the eldest sibling, Connor, struggles for relevance, while middle siblings Kendall and Shiv battle for control, and the youngest, Roman, masks insecurity with humor. The show brilliantly captures how sibling roles influence power, confidence, and communication.

Similarly, *Encanto* showcases the pressure placed on different family members—eldest sister Isabela is expected to be perfect, while middle child Luisa bears the weight of responsibility, and Mirabel, the youngest, struggles to find her place. These portrayals reflect real-life family roles and how they shape our expectations of ourselves and each other.

## The Way We Communicate Love

Every family has its own way of expressing love, and Sarah and Trey's family was no exception. In our house, conversations could be lively, passionate, even intense at times—but never without love.

Disagreements weren't battles to win or lose; they were opportunities to challenge, to understand, and to grow. No matter how heated a discussion became, the foundation of support never wavered.

Maybe that's why, despite a lifetime of deep and sometimes difficult conversations, Trey and I have never actually had a conflict.

We've had hard conversations. We've challenged each other, pushed each other to think differently, and worked through moments of frustration. But never once have we questioned our foundation. Because when love and respect are at the center, there is nothing to 'fight' over—only opportunities to support, challenge, and strengthen each other.

That doesn't mean we always agree. There have been plenty of moments where we saw the same situation from completely different angles. But instead of turning those moments into fights, we turned them into conversations—ones that made us both better.

And the more I learned about communication, the more I realized this wasn't just about us, it was about something we had been taught our whole lives. Our family never really fought. Instead, we turned arguments into "betterments." Even the hardest conversations felt like a loving friend asking, *"How can I encourage you to pursue a better version of yourself?"*

It wasn't until I spent time at friends' houses that I realized this wasn't everyone's experience.

At some sleepovers, I noticed how certain families avoided tough conversations altogether, tiptoeing around tension rather than addressing it. In others, disagreements felt heavy, like a storm rolling in—thick with tension, as if every argument threatened the relationship itself.

It made me reflect: What shapes the way we communicate? And how much of it is a choice?

As we move through this book, we're going to dive deeper into this idea—how the way we communicate shapes our relationships and how we can take control of that process.

Why do some conversations feel so hard? We'll explore why certain topics trigger us—and why avoiding them often makes things worse.

What communication habits have we inherited? Some of them serve us. Some of them hold us back. We'll break them down so you can decide what to keep and what to change.

How can we challenge someone in a way that strengthens, not damages, the relationship? We'll talk about the difference between healthy tension and unnecessary conflict.

What do we do when words or actions create distance? Sometimes, repair is necessary—and learning how to reconnect is just as important as learning how to communicate well.

*But before we go there, let's start with you.*

**Think About It:** Consider your family's communication style. Was love woven into your conversations, even the difficult ones? Were disagreements met with curiosity, avoidance, or frustration?

When you think about the relationships that matter most to you, what do you want to carry forward—and what do you want to change?

Now, think about your own role in the way you communicate. Are you reinforcing the patterns you grew up with? Or are you intentionally shaping something different?

The way we communicate isn't just something we inherit. It's something we build, moment by moment, conversation by conversation. And that means you have the power to create something even stronger—something rooted in love, understanding, and the kind of connection that lasts.

## How Birth Order Shapes Personality and Communication

Have you ever wondered why your older sibling seems more organized, or why your youngest cousin always steals the spotlight?

According to psychologist Alfred Adler, birth order plays a significant role in shaping personality and behavior—though, like most theories, it comes with nuance. Adler believed that our family role—the oldest, the middle, the youngest, or the only child—could influence how we develop our identity and how we interact with others.

Firstborns, for example, are often described as responsible, achievement-driven, and natural leaders. They grow up in a world of adults and may be more accustomed to structure and expectation. Middle children, in contrast, often become skilled diplomats—peacekeepers who learn to navigate both up and down the family hierarchy. They may also wrestle with feeling overlooked. Youngest siblings are frequently seen as charming, free-spirited, and more willing to push boundaries, often benefitting from a more relaxed parenting style. And then there are only children, who tend to be mature beyond their years, comfortable in adult company, and deeply independent.

While these patterns are widely recognized and often ring true anecdotally, modern research offers some caution. Personality development is incredibly complex, and factors like parental involvement, socioeconomic context, genetics, and even family size play a much greater role than birth order alone.

In other words, while your place in the family tree might influence your communication tendencies—like how assertive you are in group settings or how you handle feedback—it's far from a fixed destiny.

## Cultural Differences in Family Communication

Just as birth order might shape the way we see ourselves within our families, **culture** plays a profound role in how families communicate. In fact, the way we talk to our parents, resolve conflict with siblings, or make major life decisions is often deeply rooted in the cultural values we've absorbed.

In collectivist cultures—such as those in Japan, India, and many Latin American countries—family is viewed as a tightly woven unit.

There's often an emphasis on duty, loyalty, and respect for elders. Children may be raised in multigenerational households where hierarchy is observed and communication is more indirect. A child might hesitate to challenge a parent's decision, not because they lack opinions, but because questioning authority could be seen as disrespectful.

In contrast, individualist cultures—like those in the U.S., Canada, and much of Western Europe—tend to encourage independence, personal choice, and emotional expressiveness. Children in these cultures may be taught to speak up, ask questions, and assert themselves as they grow. Open dialogue between generations is often encouraged, and it's not uncommon for children to negotiate or even debate family rules.

Neither approach is "better" or "worse"—they simply reflect different worldviews. However, understanding these cultural frameworks can help us communicate across differences with more empathy and intention. For example, if you've ever felt misunderstood in a conversation with a family member who grew up in a different cultural context, it might be less about the words you used and more about the values beneath them.

## Consider the Asian Concept of Filial Piety (Respect for Elders)

In many Western families, children are encouraged to be independent, while in Asian cultures, the concept of filial piety emphasizes deep respect and duty toward parents.

In countries like China, Japan, and India, it's common for multiple generations to live under one roof, with younger members expected to care for aging parents. This difference in family dynamics affects how people communicate—many Asian cultures prioritize indirect communication and harmony, while Western families may encourage open debate.

Understanding these differences helps us navigate family relationships across cultural lines.

## Parenting Styles and Their Long-Term Effects

Whether we realize it or not, the way we were parented has a profound impact on how we show up in relationships—how we express emotions, respond to conflict, and even how we set boundaries. Psychologists generally group parenting into four main styles, each with its own unique set of long-term effects on personality and communication.

**Authoritative parents** are often seen as the ideal blend—offering high warmth alongside firm discipline. These parents set clear expectations but also create space for their children to express themselves. As a result, kids raised in this environment often grow up confident, emotionally aware, and socially skilled. They learn to communicate with respect *and* self-assurance, knowing their voice matters.

**Authoritarian parenting**, by contrast, tends to emphasize rules and discipline over emotional connection. There is less warmth and more control. While this approach can lead to obedient behavior in the short term, it can also foster anxiety, low self-esteem, or eventual rebellion—especially if children feel like they're never quite "good enough." As adults, these individuals may struggle with assertiveness or find it difficult to speak up in emotionally charged situations.

**Permissive parents** fall on the opposite end of the discipline spectrum. They offer plenty of love and support, but often avoid setting firm boundaries. Children raised in permissive homes might feel deeply cared for, but may also struggle with structure, responsibility, and accountability. In adulthood, this can show up as difficulty with follow-through or discomfort in relationships that require compromise and delayed gratification.

Then there's the **neglectful parenting style**—characterized by low warmth and low involvement. In these environments, children often grow up feeling emotionally unseen or unsupported. This can have lasting effects on their ability to regulate emotions, trust others, and establish a secure sense of self-worth. Their adult communication may be marked by withdrawal, defensiveness, or overcompensation.

Of course, no parent is perfect, and no child's experience can be captured in a single category. But reflecting on how we were raised helps us better understand why we communicate the way we do—and empowers us to break cycles that no longer serve us.

## Breaking Cycles: Healing from Toxic Family Dynamics

For many people, family is a source of love, laughter, and deep emotional roots. But for others, it can also carry a legacy of pain—patterns of emotional manipulation, boundary violations, or persistent criticism. Healing from toxic family dynamics isn't easy, but it is possible—and it often begins with awareness.

The first step is recognizing unhealthy patterns. This might include feeling guilt-tripped into decisions, being dismissed or invalidated, or constantly walking on eggshells around certain family members. These aren't just "personality quirks"—they're signs of relational habits that can erode a person's confidence and emotional safety over time.

From there, healing often means setting and maintaining boundaries, even if it feels uncomfortable. This doesn't require cutting people out of your life entirely (though in some cases, that may be necessary). It simply means learning how to say, "This is what I need to feel safe and respected," and standing by it. That process can feel awkward or even selfish at first—but in truth, it's a radical act of self-care and maturity.

For many, working through these patterns also involves **seeking outside support**—from therapists, support groups, faith communities, or trusted friends. Having people outside the family system who can affirm your experience is often key to untangling the emotional web of guilt, shame, and obligation.

Healing doesn't mean pretending everything is fine. It means telling the truth, learning to differentiate love from control, and choosing your future over your past.

## Beyond Traditional Family Structures: The Role of Chosen Families

In a world that's growing more complex and diverse, the traditional definition of family is expanding. For many people—particularly in the LGBTQIA+ community, or for those who have experienced estrangement, trauma, or deep misalignment with their biological relatives—**chosen family** becomes the lifeline. These are the friends, mentors, roommates, and community members who show up, see you, and love you without condition.

Sociologist Kath Weston famously called chosen families "families we choose," challenging the idea that only blood ties can form deep, lifelong bonds. And it's true—chosen families often provide the very emotional support, belonging, and affirmation that biological families may not be equipped or willing to offer. These relationships are no less real, no less binding, and in many ways, no less sacred.

When we broaden our understanding of family, we allow more people to feel seen. We stop measuring connection by DNA, and start measuring it by presence, kindness, trust, and shared growth. In today's world, that's more important than ever.

### Think About It:
Have you ever created a chosen family? What did that experience teach you about connection, belonging, and emotional safety?

**Stories of Family Healing and Reconciliation**
Of course, not every family story ends in distance or silence. Many people find ways to rebuild broken connections—sometimes slowly, sometimes unexpectedly, and often with great courage. Real-life stories of reconciliation remind us that even painful family histories can become places of transformation.

In her memoir *Becoming*, Michelle Obama reflects on her parents with deep affection, even as she explores the generational and cultural tensions she faced growing up. She honors their sacrifices while still being honest about the ways her world—and her values—evolved beyond theirs.

Actor Dwayne "The Rock" Johnson has also spoken publicly about repairing his relationship with his father. After years of emotional distance and hardship, Johnson chose to forgive and reconnect—acknowledging his father's complexity and finding peace in the process.

Comedian Trevor Noah's memoir *Born a Crime* tells a more layered story of survival, resistance, and resilience. Raised in apartheid South Africa by a fiercely protective mother and an abusive stepfather, Noah writes about love and fear coexisting within the same family.

His journey of defining his identity—and redefining what love and safety should look like—is a powerful reminder that healing doesn't always mean reunion. Sometimes it means clarity. Sometimes it means boundaries. But it always means growth.

## Talking Across Generations: Bridging the Gap

One of the most consistent sources of communication breakdown—especially within families—is the generational divide. The world our parents or grandparents grew up in may feel worlds away from the one we now inhabit. Technology, education, mental health awareness, and shifting cultural norms all play a role in widening that gap.

*So how do we bridge it?*

Start with active listening. Before jumping in to correct or debate, take a breath and ask, "What do they really believe? And why might they see things this way?" You don't have to agree—but understanding someone's perspective is often the first step to being heard in return.

Find common ground. Shared values—like wanting what's best for the family, the importance of hard work, or a desire to be respected—often transcend political or cultural differences. Starting there can soften defensiveness and make tough conversations more fruitful.

And finally, educate with patience. If you're talking about topics like mental health, gender identity, or generational trauma, facts can help—but stories often land more deeply. Share your experiences instead of lecturing. Invite curiosity instead of demanding agreement.

Bridging the gap is slow work—but it's also sacred work. It's where empathy, growth, and generational healing begin.

## How Different Generations Communicate
Every generation is shaped by the world it grew up in—and that includes how we communicate. Baby Boomers often favor phone calls and face-to-face conversations, valuing formality and consistency.

Gen X tends to appreciate directness and independence, with a practical, no-nonsense communication style.

Millennials grew up during the tech boom and tend to favor texting, email, and emotionally expressive communication.

Gen Z, the first truly digital-native generation, often communicates in short-form content, video, and text-based platforms—blending humor, vulnerability, and authenticity in new and creative ways.

Misunderstandings happen when these styles clash. A grandparent may misread a short text as cold. A younger employee may view a formal email as distant. But when we recognize these generational tendencies, we can adapt with empathy. It's not about changing who we are—it's about finding ways to meet each other halfway.

## How Socioeconomic Backgrounds Shape Communication
Our communication styles don't form in a vacuum—they're shaped by the environments we grow up in, and one of the biggest influences is our socioeconomic background.

From the words we choose to the expectations we hold in conversation, class culture matters. Research shows that individuals from working-class backgrounds often emphasize collective values: sharing resources, helping each other out, and working together to get through hard times. Communication in these communities may reflect interdependence and humility—where speaking too assertively might feel boastful, and offering help is a natural extension of relationship.

On the flip side, people raised in middle- or upper-class environments are often socialized to value self-expression, independence, and confidence. In these spaces, you're encouraged to "advocate for yourself," speak directly, and assert your ideas—skills that are often rewarded in educational and professional settings.

But here's the challenge: when these different communication styles meet—whether in friendships, classrooms, or romantic relationships—they can cause unspoken friction. A working-class student might see a classmate's confidence as arrogance. A manager from an affluent background might misread a quieter employee's collaborative approach as lack of initiative. Neither person is wrong—they're just speaking from different worlds.

The more we recognize how class culture shapes our ways of relating, the better equipped we are to build bridges instead of walls. Understanding doesn't erase differences—but it does replace assumptions with empathy.

**Understanding Trauma's Impact on Communication**
Sometimes silence isn't just awkward—it's protective. People who have lived through trauma—whether from childhood experiences, unhealthy relationships, or systemic oppression—often communicate differently. They might pull back, seem overly guarded, or freeze up in moments of intensity. This isn't about being "difficult" or "too sensitive"—it's about survival.

According to trauma expert Bessel van der Kolk, trauma can shape the nervous system in ways that alter how people engage with the world. Some may become hypervigilant—reading every facial expression as a threat.

Others may numb out or dissociate, struggling to articulate how they feel or even what they need. For someone who's experienced betrayal or abandonment, vulnerability can feel dangerous, not healing.

That's why trauma-informed communication is important. It means approaching conversations with gentleness, not urgency. It means listening without pressuring. And it means understanding that sometimes, giving someone space is the most compassionate thing you can do.

So if someone you care about seems hard to reach—don't push harder. Instead, offer a calm, steady presence. Say, *"I'm here when you're ready."* That kind of safety is what builds trust—and trust is the language trauma survivors understand best.

**Understanding, Healing, and Moving Forward**
Family dynamics are complicated. For some of us, family is a haven of safety and unconditional love. For others, it's a space that has required boundary-setting, unlearning, or even distance. Sometimes, we're nurturing close relationships. Other times, we're recovering from painful ones.

But in every case, the more we understand our origins—how our class background, culture, trauma history, and family roles shape us—the more empowered we become to choose our path forward.

You are not bound by the communication habits you inherited. You get to evolve. You get to repair. You get to create new patterns, speak new truths, and offer new kinds of connection to the people you love—and to yourself.

Because healing isn't just about what happened in the past. It's about who you're becoming now—and how you choose to relate moving forward.

## *Chapter Six Reflection Questions*

1. What's one phrase, rule, or "unspoken truth" you absorbed growing up that still influences how you communicate today? Is it helping you—or holding you back?
2. In your family, how was love typically expressed? Through words? Service? Silence? How has that shaped the way you give or receive love now?
3. Have you ever felt like you had to "translate" your communication style in order to be heard by someone from a different generation, class, or cultural background? What did that feel like?
4. Which parenting style most reflects your experience growing up? How has that affected your confidence, boundaries, or ability to express your needs?
5. Did your family avoid conflict, confront it directly, or process it indirectly (e.g., through humor or passive comments)? How does that influence your response to tension today?
6. When have you experienced power dynamics in a family conversation? Did you feel empowered to speak, or silenced? Why?
7. Think of a family moment that challenged you but ultimately helped you grow. What changed in you as a result of that experience?

## *Chapter Six Challenges*

1. Family Map Rewrite: Sketch a quick "family map"— not of names and relationships, but of communication styles. Who is the fixer? The silent one? The emotional one? Then, next to your name, write how you usually respond. Now ask yourself: *Is this the role I want to keep playing?*
2. Break One Cycle: Choose one communication pattern in your family you'd like to change (e.g., sarcasm, avoidance, emotional shutdown, unsolicited advice). For one week, practice showing up differently. Be the interruption to the cycle.
3. Cross-Generational Curiosity: Pick one family member from a different generation and ask them a question you've never asked before. (Try: "What was your biggest fear when you were my age?" or "What did love look like in your family growing up?") Listen with zero judgment.
4. Reclaim Your Voice: If you grew up feeling like your voice didn't matter, try this: in a conversation this week, share your opinion without apologizing for it. No "sorry, but…"—just clarity and calm confidence.
5. Generational Bridge Moment: The next time you're frustrated with a parent or elder, pause. Instead of reacting, ask, *"What were they taught about this?"* Then try reframing your response with compassion and boundary.

# Chapter 7:

# Friendship in the Modern World

*"Growing apart doesn't change the fact that for a long time we grew side by side; our roots will always be tangled."*
— *Ally Condie*

**How Do Friendships Evolve Over Time?**
Friendships are among the most defining relationships in our lives. But unlike family or romantic partnerships, friendships don't come with a clear set of rules or expectations.

Some friendships last a lifetime, while others fade due to distance, life changes, or shifting priorities. How do we navigate these changes while keeping meaningful connections alive?

In this chapter, we explore how friendships evolve, the impact of digital communication on social bonds, and the bittersweet reality of letting go when a friendship no longer serves us.

## Pop Culture Example: Childhood vs. Adult Friendships in *Toy Story* & *The Office*

One of the best depictions of friendship evolution is found in *Toy Story*. Woody and Buzz's bond starts with rivalry, deepens through shared experiences, and eventually faces the reality of growing apart. As Andy transitions to adulthood, he outgrows his toys—not because he loves them less, but because life moves forward.

Similarly, in *The Office*, Jim and Dwight's relationship shifts from workplace rivalry to an unlikely but deeply loyal friendship. Their arc reminds us that friendships can change and strengthen in unexpected ways when given the right conditions.

## Friendships Change

Sarah has a dear friend she's known since freshman year of college. They initially connected because they joined the same sorority and didn't have an established clique of friends going in. They quickly discovered they were in the same major and became fast friends. Over the course of their decades long friendship they have only lived in the same city for two years of college and another two years later into adulthood, but have continued to work to maintain the relationship across distance, seasons of life, and life challenges. They often marvel at the unlikely path their friendship took. There were several others in their friend group who moved on and lost touch. There was no major event that ended these other relationships, they just simply lost touch.

**Think About It:** Think about a friendship that has changed over time. Did it grow stronger, or did it fade? What factors contributed to the shift?

## The Stages of Friendship from Childhood to Adulthood

Friendships, like us, change as we grow. What we need from our friends as children isn't the same as what we need in our twenties—or our forties. Psychologists often describe three primary stages of friendship, each shaped by different emotional and social needs.

In childhood, friendships tend to form around convenience and shared play. We become friends with the kid who lives down the street, sits next to us in class, or shares our love for recess games and cartoon characters. At this stage, friendships are often based on proximity and shared activities more than emotional depth.

As we move into adolescence and young adulthood, friendships take on a new role. They become places of emotional support and identity formation. Our friends help us figure out who we are, what we value, and where we belong. We stay up late talking about dreams, doubts, and heartbreaks. These friendships are often intense, sometimes messy, and deeply formative.

By the time we reach adulthood, friendships shift again. They become more selective—based not just on shared interests, but on shared values, life priorities, and mutual effort.

As work, family, and personal responsibilities pile up, we no longer have the time or emotional bandwidth for every friend from every season. Therefore, we prioritize those who feel life-giving, those who "get it," and those who show up when it matters.

## What Makes Friendships Last?
Not all friendships are meant to last forever—and that's okay. But some do endure, lasting for decades and weathering all kinds of life changes.

So what's the secret? Research points to three key ingredients that often distinguish long-term friendships from those that fade.

The first is reciprocity—a balanced give-and-take between both people. Healthy friendships involve shared effort, emotional investment, and the ability to both support and be supported.

The second is shared life paths. Friendships often last longer when your lives continue to move in similar directions. It's not about having the same job or living in the same place, but about feeling understood because your seasons of life are somewhat aligned.

And finally, there's the power of emotional history and nostalgia. Longtime friends carry your past with them. They've seen you grow, fall apart, rebuild, and become someone new. Even if you don't talk every day, that shared emotional timeline can hold the friendship together through change and distance.

## The Impact of Digital Friendships and Social Media
Technology has completely transformed the way we build and maintain friendships. In many ways, its been a gift. Digital platforms allow us to stay in touch with people who live across the country or across the world. We can reconnect with old classmates, keep up with life updates, and build meaningful relationships with people we've never met in person.

But social media also comes with its complications. It can give us the illusion of closeness without the depth. A "like" or heart emoji might feel like connection, but it doesn't always replace a real conversation or a face-to-face check-in. Over time, these surface-level interactions can trick us into thinking we're maintaining friendships when those connections may be weakening beneath the algorithm.

## Dunbar's Number: How Many Friends Can We Really Maintain?

Anthropologist Robin Dunbar proposed a theory—often referred to as *Dunbar's Number*—suggesting that humans can only maintain about 150 meaningful relationships at any given time. That includes everyone from your closest inner circle to your more casual acquaintances. But within that larger group, there are layers.

According to Dunbar, most people have about five core friends—your inner circle, the ones you confide in most and trust implicitly. Next, there are 15 strong connections, which include close friends and family you rely on. Then come 50 good acquaintances, people you know well and enjoy but aren't deeply involved with. Finally, you have around 150 total social relationships, beyond which most connections become too superficial to maintain consistently.

This theory explains why scrolling through hundreds of Instagram stories might feel overwhelming. We're wired for meaningful connection, not mass connection. And while technology can expand our reach, it doesn't change the limits of our emotional bandwidth. Deep, lasting friendships still require presence, time, and genuine care—whether online or in person.

## Cultural Differences in Friendship Expectations

Friendship norms vary significantly across cultures, shaping how students connect with family, peers, and romantic partners. On a college campus, these cultural expectations can lead to misunderstandings—or provide a powerful opportunity to grow in empathy and self-awareness.

*Collectivist Cultures* (e.g., Japan, India, Latin America): In collectivist cultures, relationships often emphasize loyalty, interdependence, and a strong sense of duty—not just to friends, but to family and romantic partners as well.

**Family:** Students from collectivist cultures may check in with their families daily or feel obligated to prioritize family needs over campus activities. They might skip events or social outings to take care of family responsibilities, even from afar.

**Peers:** They may expect close friends to "stick together" consistently, offer emotional support, and invest deeply in the relationship. Group loyalty is seen as a marker of respect.

**Dating:** Romantic relationships may be approached with long-term commitment in mind from the start, and expectations may include involving family or navigating decisions communally rather than individually.

*Individualist Cultures* (e.g., U.S., Canada, Western Europe): In contrast, individualist cultures prioritize independence, personal choice, and emotional self-sufficiency.

**Family:** Students may go days or weeks without contacting family and view college as a time to "find themselves" apart from parental influence.

**Peers:** Friendships may be more situational—centered around shared classes, sports, or residence halls. If circumstances change, the friendship may naturally fade without a sense of betrayal.

**Dating:** Romantic relationships may start casually, and personal boundaries or autonomy are emphasized. Discussing future plans or involving family early might feel premature or intrusive.

Altogether, it is important to note that what feels like *loyalty* to one person might feel like *pressure* to another. What seems like *independence* to one might feel like *distance* or even *disinterest* to someone else.

Recognizing these cultural frameworks can help students be more patient, curious, and compassionate in their relationships.

## How Gender Shapes Conflict Styles

Research suggests that men and women often approach conflict differently due to social conditioning. Studies show that men are more likely to engage in direct, solution-focused communication, while women may prioritize relational harmony and emotional expression (Tannen, 1990).

However, these patterns are shifting as more workplaces and relationships emphasize emotional intelligence and balanced communication. Recognizing these differences can help us navigate conflicts with greater awareness and empathy.

### Are Online Friendships Real Friendships?

While virtual friendships are "less real" than in-person ones, research suggests they can still be beneficial. Studies show that online relationships can offer deep emotional support, especially for marginalized individuals who struggle to find acceptance in their physical communities (McKenna & Bargh, 2000). A late-night video call or a heartfelt message can hold just as much weight as an in-person coffee date. The medium matters less than the intention behind it. Online friendships require the same level of honesty, trust, and investment to truly thrive. However, they also come with unique challenges, such as misinterpretations, ghosting, and lack of nonverbal cues.

**Think About It:** Have you ever felt closer to someone you met online than someone in real life? What factors made that connection feel real?

### Who Does the Emotional Work in Relationships?

In many relationships—romantic, familial, or professional—women and marginalized groups often take on emotional labor, meaning they are expected to manage emotions, mediate conflicts, and provide emotional support (Hochschild, 1983).

This unspoken expectation can lead to frustration, resentment, and burnout. Open conversations about balancing emotional responsibilities can create healthier, more equitable relationships.

**Think About It:** Have you ever felt like you were doing more "emotional work" than the other person in a relationship? How can these responsibilities be more fairly distributed?

## *Chapter Seven Reflection Questions*

1. Think of a friendship that has changed since high school or your first year of college. What caused the shift, and how did it affect you?
2. Have you ever maintained a meaningful friendship entirely online or at a distance? What made it work—or not?
3. Which friendship stage (childhood, adolescence, adulthood) do you think has shaped your understanding of what it means to be a "true friend" the most?
4. How do you personally define friendship? Has your definition changed as you've grown?
5. Have you ever been in a friendship where the emotional labor felt one-sided? How did you navigate it—or how do you wish you had?
6. Social media keeps us connected, but does it make you feel closer to your friends or more distant? Why?
7. How has your cultural background or upbringing shaped your expectations of friendship, loyalty, and boundaries?
8. Who are your "inner five" people right now—the ones you trust most? How often do you show them appreciation?
9. Have you ever struggled to let go of a friendship that no longer served you? What made that decision difficult or freeing?
10. If someone were to describe *you* as a friend, what would you hope they'd say? What would they *actually* say?

## *Chapter Seven Challenges*

1. Choose one friend who has made a difference in your life and write them a short message, text, or voice note expressing why they matter to you. Be specific.
2. Spend one day limiting passive interaction (likes, scrolling) and instead initiate three meaningful digital or in-person connections.
3. Revisit an old friendship—send a message to someone you haven't talked to in over a year. See where it leads, even if it's just a kind check-in.
4. Audit your own "Dunbar's number." Who are your five closest people? Your next 15? Make a list and reflect on how often you're showing up for them.
5. Try scheduling a phone or video chat instead of texting with a close friend this week. Notice how the connection feels different when you hear their voice.
6. If there's a friendship you've been questioning, journal about whether it's time to nurture it—or let it go. Be honest with yourself.
7. Host a "low-key friend night" (even if it's just two people). No agenda, just time to talk, listen, and laugh.
8. Pay attention to your emotional labor in friendships. Are you always the one planning, checking in, or calming tension? Try asking for what you need, too.
9. Learn how friendships work in a culture different from your own. Watch a short video or read an article—and reflect on what surprises you.

# Chapter 8:

# The Dynamics of Romantic Relationships

*"Love is not about how many days, months, or years you have been together. It's all about how much you love each other every single day."*
— *Unknown*

**What Makes Romantic Relationships Last?**
Romantic relationships are among the most intense and rewarding connections we experience. They bring companionship, passion, and deep emotional intimacy—but they also come with challenges.

Why do some relationships last a lifetime while others fall apart? What roles do communication, attachment, and shared effort play in building a strong romantic partnership?

In this chapter, we explore the formation, maintenance, and challenges of romantic relationships, looking at the science behind love and the real-life strategies that help relationships thrive.

## The Evolution of a Love Story (*The Notebook* vs. *How I Met Your Mother*)

Few love stories capture the highs and lows of a lifelong romance like *The Notebook*. Noah and Allie's relationship is defined by deep passion, struggles, and ultimately, unwavering commitment. It's a classic portrayal of enduring love despite challenges.

On the other hand, *How I Met Your Mother* offers a more modern, sometimes messy look at love. Ted's romantic journey shows how expectations, timing, and personal growth influence relationships.

While some relationships stand the test of time, others dissolve—not necessarily because of a lack of love, but because life takes people in different directions.

## The Role of Communication in a Lasting Relationship

As professors, we have seen countless young adults navigating the complexities of romantic relationships—balancing school, work, and personal ambitions. Unfortunately, it doesn't get any easier once you're on the other side of the educational experience.

In our own experiences, we've learned that open, honest communication is the single most important factor in making a relationship work. Small misunderstandings can snowball into larger conflicts when left unaddressed, while regular check-ins and vulnerability strengthen the foundation of a partnership.

**Think About It:** Let's get real—have you ever been in a situation where something *small* blew up into something *major* because no one actually talked about it? Maybe a "left on read" text turned into an awkward week. Or maybe the lack of a simple, honest conversation slowly unraveled something meaningful.

When has communication (or the lack of it) made or broken a romantic relationship in your life—or in the life of someone close to you? What could've been said earlier? What *was* said that really stuck? What did silence communicate? Whether it happened face-to-face or over text, think about the role communication played—and what you'd do differently next time.

Romantic relationships can feel confusing. Whether you've been in one, are figuring one out, or have just watched the drama unfold in your friend group or favorite show, it's clear that love isn't always straightforward. But there is good news. Researchers have actually spent decades studying what makes romantic relationships tick. So while love can feel like a mystery, there's real science behind the emotions, choices, and patterns that shape how we connect.

### *The Stages of Romantic Relationships*
Psychologists suggest that romantic relationships often unfold in five key stages, each offering its own blend of emotions, challenges, and opportunities for growth. The journey typically begins with **Attraction and Infatuation**—commonly known as the honeymoon phase. In this stage, partners are drawn together by chemistry, curiosity, and excitement. Everything feels new, intense, and hopeful.

But as time passes, this initial glow naturally gives way to the **Reality Check**. During this stage, differences in values, habits, and communication styles begin to surface. It's here that partners must learn how to navigate conflict, manage expectations, and move beyond idealized images of one another.

If a couple successfully works through this second stage, they often enter the **Commitment and Growth** phase. Here, trust deepens, and love becomes more about choosing each other intentionally—not just emotionally.

Partners begin to actively invest in each other's lives and dreams, facing life's challenges side by side. This sets the stage for **Maturity and Stability**, a period defined by emotional security, shared routines, and a sense of long-term partnership.

The final stage—**Evolution or Dissolution**—acknowledges the reality that not all relationships last forever. Some couples grow together, adapting through life's transitions, while others drift apart or choose to part ways.

The difference between fleeting passion and enduring love often lies in how a couple transitions from infatuation to true companionship.

### Attachment Theory and Romantic Compatibility

As we reviewed in a previous chapter, our early childhood experiences play a profound role in shaping how we love and connect as adults. According to attachment theory, we develop internal models of trust, intimacy, and vulnerability based on our relationships with caregivers.

Let's take a closer look at how these early templates often reappear in adult romantic relationships in the form of distinct attachment styles.

Individuals with a **Secure Attachment** style are typically comfortable with both intimacy and independence, making them reliable and emotionally balanced partners.

Those with an **Anxious Attachment** style often crave closeness but may become overly concerned with rejection or abandonment, leading to emotional highs and lows.

On the other end of the spectrum, people with an **Avoidant Attachment** style tend to value autonomy and may struggle with expressing emotions or relying on others.

Then there is the **Fearful-Avoidant** (or disorganized) style—a complex mix of both anxious and avoidant behaviors—characterized by both a desire for intimacy and a fear of getting hurt.

Understanding your own attachment style—and that of your partner—can dramatically improve communication and compatibility. For example, a secure individual dating someone with anxious tendencies may need to offer more consistent reassurance, while a relationship involving an avoidant partner may require patience, openness, and a willingness to discuss emotional boundaries.

Recognizing these patterns not only improves empathy but also gives partners the tools to build deeper, more supportive relationships.

**Cultural Perspectives on Romantic Relationships**
Romantic relationships don't exist in a vacuum—they are deeply influenced by the cultural contexts in which they develop. Across different parts of the world, societal values shape how love, commitment, and marriage are understood and expressed.

In Western cultures such as the United States, Canada, and much of Europe, love is often centered around personal choice, romantic attraction, and emotional fulfillment. Here, individuals typically pursue relationships that align with their own interests and identities, with less emphasis on family involvement. In contrast, Eastern and collectivist cultures, such as those in India, China, and the Middle East, tend to view relationships through the lens of family, tradition, and long-term stability. In these cultures, romantic decisions are often influenced by family approval, shared values, and a sense of duty.

## Consider Arranged Marriages vs. Love Marriages Across Cultures

While Hollywood often focuses on romantic love, many cultures value arranged marriages—where families play a role in matchmaking. Studies suggest that arranged marriages can lead to equal or even higher satisfaction rates than love marriages because they prioritize long-term compatibility over short-term passion. In contrast, Western societies emphasize choice and emotional connection.

Both models highlight the different ways relationships form across cultures, reminding us that love and connection are shaped by tradition, values, and societal norms.

Interestingly, arranged marriages have been shown to result in similar or even higher levels of marital satisfaction when compared to self-selected marriages, largely due to aligned life goals, family support, and cultural cohesion. These differences highlight how love can be both deeply personal and a reflection of broader societal expectations.

## The Foundation of Strong Romantic Relationships

No matter the attachment style or cultural background, good communication remains the bedrock of any successful romantic relationship. Research identifies three essential communication skills that help partners thrive: active listening, conflict resolution, and expressing appreciation.

**Active listening** goes beyond simply hearing words—it means truly tuning in, making eye contact, asking thoughtful questions, and resisting the urge to interrupt or immediately respond.

**Conflict resolution**, when handled respectfully, can actually strengthen a relationship. It's not about avoiding disagreements but learning how to express frustration without blame and work toward shared solutions.

**Expressing appreciation,** another crucial but often overlooked skill is, can be the small, regular acts of gratitude—like thanking your partner for making dinner, sending a kind message, or giving an unexpected compliment. These seemingly simple habits build emotional intimacy, create a sense of security, and make a powerful difference in sustaining connection over time.

## The Gottman Method: Warning Signs and Repair

Dr. John Gottman, a leading relationship researcher, developed a framework to identify the most damaging communication habits in relationships—what he calls the **Four Horsemen of the Apocalypse**.

1. Criticism: Attacking character instead of the issue.
2. Defensiveness: Avoiding responsibility, shifting blame.
3. Contempt: Mocking, belittling, showing disrespect.
4. Stonewalling: Emotionally shutting down, refusing to communicate.

According to Gottman, the frequent presence of these behaviors is a strong predictor of relationship breakdown.

However, there is hope. Gottman also emphasizes the power of **repair attempts**—small gestures like humor, a sincere apology, or a gentle touch in the middle of an argument. These acts signal a willingness to reconnect and de-escalate, even when emotions are running high. Couples who learn to repair after conflict often build resilience and deeper emotional trust over time.

### Navigating the Modern Dating Landscape
Romantic relationships in the 21st century come with unique challenges. The rise of dating apps and social media has transformed how people meet and connect. On one hand, there's unprecedented access to potential partners; on the other, this abundance can lead to what researchers call the **paradox of choice**—the more options we have, the harder it becomes to commit. This constant swiping culture can make relationships feel transactional or disposable.

Hookup culture also presents its own complexities, especially for those seeking emotional intimacy rather than just physical connection. While casual dating can be empowering for some, others may find it difficult to transition from surface-level encounters to meaningful, long-term relationships.

Additionally, **long-distance relationships** have become more common in an age of global mobility and digital communication. These relationships require intentional effort, clear communication, and trust-building rituals to thrive despite physical distance.

### Why Do We Love the Way We Do?
Think about the last time you watched a romantic movie or read a love story that stuck with you. Was it an epic, passionate romance (*Titanic*)? A long-lasting, deeply committed relationship (*Up*)? A tragic tale of love that burned fast and bright (*Romeo and Juliet*)? The reason these stories resonate so much is because love isn't just one thing—it comes in many forms.

### Sternberg's Triangular Theory of Love
Psychologist Robert Sternberg cracked the code on love by breaking it down into three key ingredients:

1. Intimacy: Emotional closeness, bonding, and trust
2. Passion: Physical attraction, excitement, and desire
3. Commitment: The conscious decision to stay together long-term

Different combinations of these elements create different types of love—some lasting, some fleeting, some built to stand the test of time. This chapter explores Sternberg's Triangular Theory of Love to help you better understand your own relationships, past and present.

**The Different Types of Love (As Seen in Hollywood)**
Love isn't one-size-fits-all. Every great love story fits somewhere on Sternberg's triangle—some are full of passion but lack depth, while others are steady and strong but missing a spark.

Let's take a tour through some of the most well-known love stories to see this theory in action.

**Romantic Love (Intimacy + Passion, No Commitment).** Ever had a love that felt magnetic and exhilarating, but it never quite reached the "forever" stage? That's romantic love—full of emotional closeness and chemistry, but without long-term commitment.

*Example: Jack & Rose in Titanic.* They were crazy about each other, shared deep emotional moments, and had undeniable chemistry—but there wasn't time for commitment before, well... the iceberg.

**Fatuous Love (Passion + Commitment, No Intimacy).** This is the "whirlwind romance"—people jump into a relationship based on passion and a strong desire to be together, but they don't have deep emotional intimacy.

*Example: Romeo & Juliet.* They barely knew each other, yet were all in, fast. They skipped intimacy and emotional depth, committing without truly understanding each other.

Quick Marriages for Security. In some cultures, marriages happen quickly due to family expectations or religious beliefs. Passion and commitment might be there, but emotional intimacy may take time to develop.

**Companionate Love (Intimacy + Commitment, No Passion).** This is a deep friendship that lasts a lifetime. It may be a long-term romance that has lost passion, but it still has emotional closeness and a strong commitment.

*Example: Carl & Ellie in Up.* They were each other's best friends, their love deepened over time, and they remained devoted to each other. Even though their love wasn't fiery and passionate later in life, their bond were unshakable.

Arranged Marriages That Grow into Deep Love – In many cultures, arranged marriages start with commitment first, and intimacy grows over time. These relationships often thrive when partners build emotional trust and connection.

**Empty Love (Commitment Only, No Passion or Intimacy).** This is the love that feels like a contract, not a connection—a marriage or long-term partnership that has lost both emotional closeness and passion but remains intact due to obligation or convenience.

*Example: Loveless Marriages in Period Dramas.* Think of arranged royal marriages (*Bridgerton*, *The Crown*) where commitment is there, but there's little real love.

*Real-World Example:* Long-Term Couples Who Stay Together "For the Kids." Many people stay in relationships out of duty or financial security, even if the emotional and passionate elements have faded.

**Consummate Love (Intimacy + Passion + Commitment) – The Ultimate Goal.** This is the holy grail of love—the one that lasts, the one that thrives, the one we all dream of. It has emotional depth (intimacy), fiery chemistry (passion), and an unwavering bond (commitment).

*Example: The Notebook's Noah & Allie.* They fought, they loved fiercely, they stayed together through thick and thin. Even when Allie forgot Noah due to Alzheimer's, his commitment to her never wavered.

**Lifelong Love Across Different Cultures**
Many couples across the world work hard to nurture all three elements—some arrange "date nights" to reignite passion, some work through struggles to keep commitment strong, and some prioritize emotional closeness through daily connection.

Ask Yourself: Is it possible to have all three in one relationship? Have you ever experienced a love that had one or two of these elements but not all three?

**Love Evolves—And That's a Good Thing**
Sternberg's theory isn't just about labeling love—it's about understanding that love is fluid and ever-changing. The best relationships adapt, grow, and shift over time.

## *Hollywood's Relationship Rollercoaster*

As we learned in a previous chapter, the Relational Stages Model explains how relationships form, grow, and sometimes dissolve. Relationships in movies and TV shows often closely follow Knapp's model. Let's look at some iconic examples to see these stages in action.

- Harry & Sally (*When Harry Met Sally*). A slow progression through all the stages, moving from friendship to love, with plenty of ups and downs.
- Jim & Pam (*The Office*). From their first interactions as coworkers to deep emotional intimacy, commitment, and (almost) a breakdown, they follow Knapp's model step by step.
- Ross & Rachel (*Friends*). The ultimate example of coming together, falling apart, and finding their way back (over ten seasons).

## Coming Together: The Growth of a Relationship

Let's take a closer look at Knapp's Relationship Stages in the context of romantic partners.

***1. Initiating: The First Impression.*** This is the moment of first contact—a glance across the room, a handshake at work, a match on a dating app. It's all about first impressions, deciding if you want to take things further.

*Example: The First Meet-Cute* – When Elizabeth Bennet and Mr. Darcy meet in *Pride and Prejudice*, their first impression is rocky, but that's just the beginning.

Arranged Marriages & Cultural Norms – In some cultures, the first stage of a relationship isn't necessarily about attraction but about family introductions and seeing if values align.

Ask Yourself: Have you ever made a snap judgment about someone in the initiating stage that later turned out to be wrong?

**2. Experimenting: Small Talk and Testing the Waters.** Now comes the getting-to-know-you phase—casual conversations, discovering common interests, seeing if there's a connection.

*Example: Kat & Patrick in 10 Things I Hate About You* – Their sarcastic banter is the classic "experimenting" stage, testing compatibility through playful (and sometimes snarky) exchanges.

When people from different cultures date, this stage might involve navigating language barriers, family expectations, and learning about different customs.

Ask Yourself: What's the best (or worst) first conversation you've had with someone?

**3. Intensifying: Emotional Closeness Grows.** Now, the connection deepens—inside jokes, personal stories, shared experiences. In romantic relationships, this is the "falling in love" stage. In friendships, it's the "best friend" stage.

*Example: Buzz & Woody in Toy Story* – They start as rivals, but as they go through challenges together, their trust grows, and they become true best friends.

Ask Yourself: What's one small moment that made you realize someone was a true friend or romantic partner?

***4. Integrating: "We" Instead of "Me".*** This is where two people's lives blend together—couples start sharing routines, friends start acting as a unit, and personal identities start overlapping.

*Example: Monica & Chandler in Friends* – When they move in together, they transition from "Monica" and "Chandler" to "Monica & Chandler," their lives fully integrated.

Ask Yourself: Have you ever had a relationship (friendship or romantic) where your identities felt merged? How did that feel?

***5. Bonding: The Ultimate Commitment.*** This is the peak of a relationship—weddings, best-friend tattoos, long-term business partnerships. It's about formalizing a commitment in a lasting way.

*Example: The Avengers* – They go from solo superheroes to a fully committed team, bound by a shared mission.

Not all deep connections form through romance or blood. Many individuals create chosen families—lifelong relationships rooted in emotional closeness, mutual support, and shared experience.

Ask Yourself: What's the strongest bond you've ever had?

## Coming Apart: When Relationships Change or End

***6. Differentiating: "You" vs. "Me"***. This is the first sign of cracks—where differences start feeling bigger than similarities.

*Example: The Breakup (Jennifer Aniston & Vince Vaughn)* – A classic case of differentiating, where every little difference starts feeling like an argument.

Ask Yourself: Have you been in a relationship and started focusing more on differences than shared experiences?

### 7. *Circumscribing: Walking on Eggshells.*
Communication starts to slow down—important topics are avoided, and people tiptoe around each other instead of addressing problems.

*Example: Meredith & Derek in Grey's Anatomy* – During their rough patches, they start talking *around* issues rather than *about* them.

Ask Yourself: Have you ever been afraid to talk about something in a relationship?

### 8. *Stagnating: The Relationship Is "There" But Not Growing.*
Nothing is really happening. No progress, no excitement—just routine, silence, and emotional distance.

*Example: Joel & Clementine in Eternal Sunshine of the Spotless Mind* – They stay in the relationship even when it's emotionally dead, feeling stuck.

Ask Yourself: Have you ever stayed in a relationship (romantic or platonic) because it felt easier than ending it?

### 9. *Avoiding: Creating Distance.*
One or both people start physically or emotionally pulling away.

*Example: Gatsby & Daisy in The Great Gatsby* – Even though Gatsby is obsessed with Daisy, she avoids fully reconnecting with him.

Ask Yourself: Have you ever had a relationship where someone started avoiding you—or vice versa?

**10. Terminating: *The Official Goodbye.*** The final stage—closure, breakups, endings. Sometimes it's mutual, sometimes it's painful, but it's a clear severing of ties.

*Example: La La Land* – Their love was real, but life took them in different directions.

Ask Yourself: Do you think all relationships need "closure," or can some endings remain open-ended?

## Forgiveness and The Science of Reconciliation

Conflict is inevitable, but how we handle repair attempts determines the strength of a relationship. Studies show that forgiveness is a process—not a one-time decision—requiring emotional processing, boundary-setting, and sometimes even mutual accountability (Worthington et al., 2016).

Instead of saying "I'm sorry *if* I hurt you" (which deflects responsibility), try "I recognize that my actions caused harm, and I want to make it right."

## Relational Dialectics Theory

Have you ever wanted closeness but also independence in a relationship? Or felt torn between sharing everything and keeping some things private? These tensions are explained by Relational Dialectics Theory (RDT) (Baxter & Montgomery, 1996).

This theory highlights three common relationship tensions:
- Autonomy vs. Connection – The need for both independence and intimacy.

- Openness vs. Privacy – The balance between transparency and personal boundaries.
- Predictability vs. Novelty – The desire for routine while also craving excitement.

Understanding that these tensions are normal—rather than signs of a failing relationship—allows partners to navigate them with communication, compromise, and mutual respect.

Quick Recap: What We've Learned So Far

- Romantic relationships evolve through distinct stages (Knapp)
- There are different types of loves, see the Triangular Theory of Love (Sternberg)
- Attachment styles influence relationship dynamics (Bowlby).
- Communication skills like active listening and conflict resolution are essential.
- The Four Horsemen of toxic communication can predict relationship breakdowns (Gottman).
- Cultural differences shape expectations around love and marriage.
- Modern dating presents unique challenges, from dating apps to long-distance connections.

As a parting thought, *love is a Choice*. Long-lasting romantic relationships aren't just built on chemistry or fate—they require intentionality, effort, and emotional investment. The happiest couples understand that love is not just a feeling but an ongoing choice to support, respect, and grow together. Relationships evolve. Understanding these stages helps us appreciate, nurture, and, when necessary, let go of connections with wisdom and grace.

## *Chapter Eight Reflection Questions*

1. Think about your attachment style. How do you think it influences your communication in romantic relationships—especially during conflict or emotional stress?
2. Have you ever witnessed a relationship that shifted types on Sternberg's Triangle of Love (e.g., from Romantic to Companionate)? What do you believe caused the shift?
3. In what ways do cultural or familial expectations influence how you think about love, commitment, or dating? Do any of these expectations feel empowering or limiting?
4. What are some common tensions (autonomy vs. connection, openness vs. privacy, etc.) you've noticed in your romantic relationships, and how have you navigated them?
5. Can you recall a moment when active listening made a positive impact on a relationship? What changed because you—or your partner—truly listened?
6. What does "consummate love" mean to you personally? Do you think it's achievable or idealized? Why or why not?
7. Have you ever witnessed one of the Four Horsemen behaviors in a relationship? How was it handled—or not handled?
8. What's your reaction to the idea that some arranged marriages report higher satisfaction than love marriages? What does that reveal about your values?
9. How has the rise of dating apps, social media, or hookup culture shaped your approach to romance or dating? Are you hopeful, skeptical, curious, or overwhelmed?

## *Chapter Eight Challenges*

1. Love Triangle Reflection. Pick three romantic relationships you've seen—one from a movie, one from real life, and one from your own experience. Map them on Sternberg's Triangle (intimacy, passion, commitment) and compare the dynamics.
2. Attachment Style Quiz + Reflection. Take a free online attachment style quiz. Write a one-paragraph reflection on how your style has shown up in past relationships—and one change you'd like to make moving forward.
3. Media Case Study. Choose a romantic relationship from TV or film (e.g., Jim & Pam, Ross & Rachel, Kat & Patrick) and break it down using Knapp's 10 stages. Present it as a timeline or visual chart.
4. Rewrite a "Horseman" Moment. Think about a time you witnessed criticism, contempt, defensiveness, or stonewalling. Rewrite the scene with a healthy repair attempt (e.g., humor, apology, gentle startup). What difference might it have made?
5. Love Languages Experiment. Learn your love language and ask a close friend or partner to do the same. For one week, intentionally practice speaking their love language (e.g., acts of service or words of affirmation) and journal what you noticed.

## *Chapter 8 Appendix: Understanding Your LOVE Story and Patterns Worksheet*

**Instructions:** Complete each section of the worksheet on the following pages, either individually or as a couple. Be honest and reflective as you analyze your relationship using three prominent relationship theories: Knapp's Relational Stages Model, Sternberg's Triangular Theory of Love, and Gottman's Four Horsemen. If you are single, reflect on a past relationship or a relationship you know well.

### Knapp's Relational Stages Model

Mark L. Knapp is a distinguished professor of communication, known for his research on interpersonal communication and nonverbal behavior. His Relational Stages Model remains one of the most widely recognized frameworks for understanding how relationships evolve. Knapp's model explains how relationships form, grow, and sometimes dissolve. It is divided into two phases: Coming Together and Coming Apart with five stages in each.

### Coming Together:
1. **Initiation** – First impressions and brief interactions.
2. **Experimentation** – Small talk and shared interests emerge.
3. **Intensifying** – Emotional closeness deepens, and trust builds.
4. **Integration** – Relationship solidifies; lives intertwine.
5. **Bonding** – Making commitment (marriage, partnership).

### Coming Apart:
1. **Differentiating** – Partners emphasize differences.
2. **Circumscribing** – Communication reduces.
3. **Stagnating** – Relationship feels stuck; little growth.
4. **Avoiding** – Physical and emotional withdrawal.
5. **Terminating** – Relationship officially ends

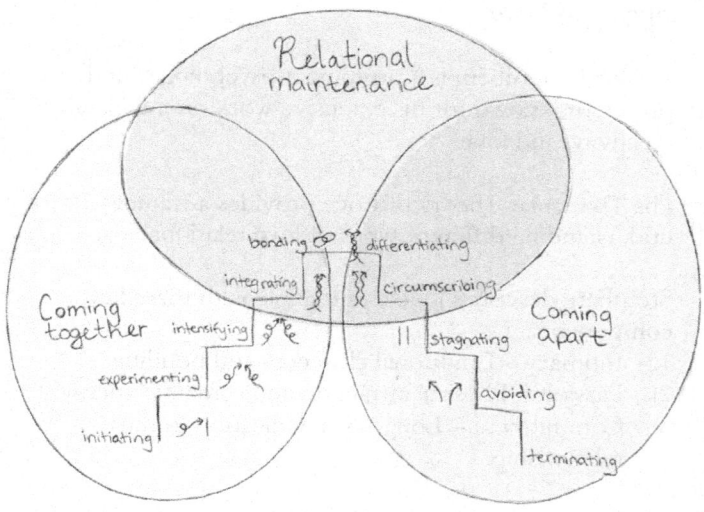

## *Knapp Reflection & Discussion Questions*

- Can you recall a time when your relationship transitioned from one stage to another? What prompted the shift?

- If you are currently in a "Coming Apart" stage, what steps could help reverse the trend?

- How do external factors (such as career changes, family dynamics, or health issues) influence movement between these stages?

## Sternberg's Triangular Theory of Love: The Building Blocks of Love

Robert J. Sternberg is a prominent psychologist and professor, known for his extensive work on intelligence, creativity, and love.

His Triangular Theory of Love provides a framework for understanding different types of love relationships.

Sternberg describes love as a triangle with three key components:
1. Intimacy – Emotional closeness and bonding.
2. Passion – Physical attraction and romantic energy.
3. Commitment – Long-term dedication to the relationship.

Different relationships exhibit different combinations of these elements, leading to types of love:
- Consummate Love (All three elements present) – The most fulfilling and enduring form of love.
- Companionate Love (Intimacy + Commitment) – Deep friendship and long-term connection.
- Romantic Love (Intimacy + Passion) – Emotionally and physically intense, but may lack longevity.
- Fatuous Love (Passion + Commitment) – Fast-moving relationships lacking deep emotional connection.

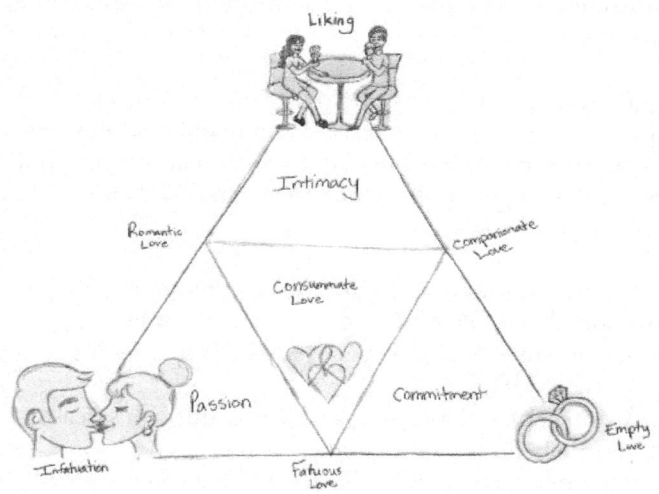

## Sternberg Reflection & Discussion Questions

- Where do you currently place your relationship on Sternberg's love triangle?

- Have you experienced shifts between different types of love in your relationship? What caused those changes?

- If you could strengthen one of the three components (intimacy, passion, or commitment), which would it be and why?

## Gottman's Four Horsemen: Identifying Destructive Patterns

Dr. John Gottman is a psychologist and relationship expert best known for his research on marital stability and divorce prediction. He founded the Gottman Institute and has developed practical, science-backed methods for improving relationships.

Gottman identifies four negative communication behaviors that predict relationship dissatisfaction:
1. **Criticism** – Attacking your partner's character instead of behavior.
2. **Contempt** – Expressing superiority through sarcasm or mockery.
3. **Defensiveness** – Refusing to take responsibility or blaming your partner.
4. **Stonewalling** – Shutting down and withdrawing from conflict.

Each horseman has an antidote:
- **Criticism** → Gentle Start-Up
- **Contempt** → Build Appreciation & Respect
- **Defensiveness** → Take Responsibility
- **Stonewalling** → Practice Self-Soothing

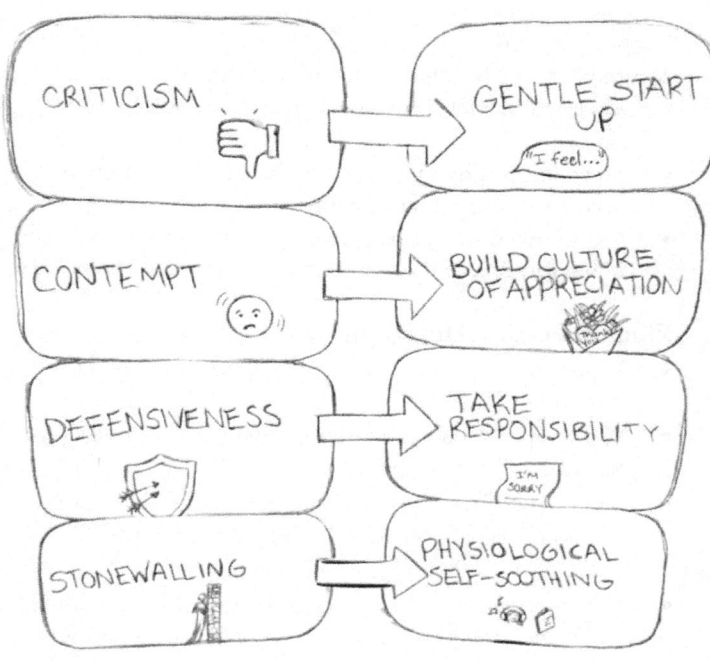

## Gottman Reflection & Discussion Questions

- Have you noticed any of the Four Horsemen in your own relationship? How do they manifest?

- What are some specific examples of how you and your partner have handled conflict in the past?

- What steps can you take to replace negative communication habits with their antidotes?

## Putting It All Together:

Each of these theories offers a different but complementary lens for understanding relationships.
- Knapp's Model shows how relationships evolve over time.
- Sternberg's Triangle explains the quality and depth of love within that relationship.
- Gottman's Four Horsemen highlight communication behaviors that either strengthen or weaken the bond.

## Final Reflection Questions:
- Where is your relationship in Knapp's model? How did you get here?
- What type of love are you experiencing according to Sternberg's Triangle?
- Have any of the Four Horsemen appeared in your relationship? How can you replace them with antidotes?
- What steps can you take to move toward Consummate Love and stay in a healthy stage of Knapp's Model?
- How do these theories together help you see your relationship more clearly?

## Final Thoughts:

Understanding relationship stages, love dynamics, and communication patterns can help you create a deeper, more fulfilling relationship.

Write a short commitment statement outlining one change you want to make for your relationship and how you plan to implement it

# Chapter 9:

# Communication in the Workplace – Building Meaningful Professional Relationships

*"The art of communication is the language of leadership."*
— James Humes

### How Does Communication Shape Success in the Workplace?

Our careers are built on more than just skills and expertise—how we communicate in professional settings can define opportunities, shape workplace culture, and impact career growth. From leadership to collaboration, from mentorship to conflict resolution, effective communication is the foundation of professional success.

But what does effective workplace communication look like? How do we navigate power dynamics, feedback, and digital communication in a world that is increasingly remote and hybrid?

In this chapter, we explore workplace communication styles, the role of mentorship, leadership strategies, and handling professional conflict, all with an eye toward building healthy, productive, and meaningful work relationships. But first let's consider some pop culture examples.

## Leadership and Communication in *Ted Lasso* and *The Devil Wears Prada*

Leadership styles in the workplace vary widely, and pop culture gives us some extreme examples. *Ted Lasso* offers a refreshing take on empathetic leadership, where coaching is built on trust, encouragement, and leading by example.

On the other hand, Miranda Priestly in *The Devil Wears Prada* embodies an authoritarian leadership style, where fear, intimidation, and hierarchy dominate.

While both approaches yield results, research suggests that leaders who communicate with emotional intelligence, rather than intimidation, create more innovative and loyal teams.

## Understanding Communication Styles in the Workplace

In any workplace, recognizing that not everyone communicates the same way is essential for fostering strong, collaborative relationships. There are four primary communication styles, each with distinct characteristics.

**Assertive communicators** express themselves clearly and respectfully, balancing confidence with empathy. They're often solution-oriented and direct in addressing concerns.

**Passive communicators,** on the other hand, tend to avoid confrontation and may struggle to advocate for themselves, often leaving issues unresolved.

**Aggressive communicators** dominate conversations and seek control, which can create tension or fear among colleagues.

Then there's the **passive-aggressive** style—marked by indirectness, sarcasm, or subtle forms of resistance—which can undermine trust and lead to miscommunication.

For example, while an assertive team member might propose a solution to a problem in a meeting, a passive colleague might stay quiet and later feel frustrated.

Understanding these communication styles not only improves everyday interactions but also builds a healthier, more respectful workplace environment.

## Leadership and Communication: The Traits of Great Leaders

Great leadership is built on more than just strong decision-making—it's rooted in effective communication. Research consistently shows that the most successful leaders share several key traits when it comes to how they interact with others. First, they prioritize clarity, ensuring that their messages are concise and easy to understand.

They also demonstrate emotional intelligence, meaning they're aware of both their own emotions and the emotional cues of those around them. Active listening is another hallmark of strong leadership—great leaders truly listen to understand, not just to respond.

Finally, they practice adaptability, adjusting their communication style to suit different audiences and situations. Leaders like Oprah Winfrey and Simon Sinek exemplify these traits. They connect deeply with others through storytelling, empathy, and intentional listening, inspiring people not just with what they say, but with how they say it.

## Consider Indra Nooyi's Leadership at PepsiCo

Great leaders aren't just effective communicators—they are emotionally intelligent. Indra Nooyi, the former CEO of PepsiCo, was known for writing personal letters to her employees' parents, thanking them for raising hardworking individuals.

This small but meaningful act deepened employee loyalty and engagement. Nooyi's leadership shows that professional communication isn't just about strategy—it's about building relationships that inspire.

## Power Dynamics and Workplace Hierarchy

Workplace communication isn't just about what's being said—it's also about who is speaking and to whom. Power dynamics significantly influence the way messages are delivered, received, and interpreted in professional settings.

When communicating with peers, the tone tends to be more collaborative, often emphasizing shared goals and collective decision-making. This kind of lateral communication helps build trust and mutual respect among coworkers. However, when speaking with managers or executives, communication must strike a careful balance between demonstrating confidence and showing respect for authority.

It's less about casual conversation and more about being intentional, strategic, and aligned with organizational priorities. On the flip side, leaders must be equally thoughtful in how they communicate. Their words carry weight, and effective leadership communication requires clarity, the ability to inspire, and a gift for offering feedback in a way that corrects without alienating.

For example, when presenting a new idea to senior leadership, framing the proposal around its impact on company goals—rather than personal enthusiasm—can increase buy-in and perceived professionalism.

## The Power of a Mentor's Words

Early in my career, I had a mentor who gave me one of the most impactful pieces of advice:

*"The way you say something is just as important as what you say."*

I had always assumed that being right was what mattered most, but I quickly learned that tone, delivery, and timing determined how my ideas were received. That single lesson reshaped how I approached workplace conversations, from delivering presentations to handling difficult feedback.

**Think About It:** Think about a time when communication at work either helped or hurt your professional growth. What did you learn from it?

## Giving and Receiving Constructive Criticism

Feedback is one of the most essential, yet frequently mishandled, forms of communication in the workplace. Done well, it can empower growth and increase trust; done poorly, it can create tension and diminish morale. One effective approach for giving feedback is the SBI method, which stands for *Situation*, *Behavior*, and *Impact*. This approach removes vague judgments and replaces them with clear, specific observations.

For instance, instead of saying, "You need to be more prepared," you might say, "In our last meeting (situation), I noticed you didn't have the key data points ready (behavior), which made it harder for the team to make decisions (impact)."

On the receiving end, it's just as important to listen actively, ask clarifying questions, and try not to respond with defensiveness. Thoughtful feedback—whether given or received—helps create a culture of accountability and growth, rather than fear or avoidance.

## Addressing Bias and Practicing Inclusive Communication

Bias—both conscious and unconscious—can deeply impact workplace communication. It influences who gets the floor in meetings, whose ideas are taken seriously, and how individuals are perceived based on gender, race, neurodiversity, and more.

Practicing inclusive communication means actively working to dismantle those barriers. It could be as simple as swapping out gendered terms like "you guys" for more inclusive language like "everyone" or "team." It also involves paying attention to speaking time in meetings—research has shown that women, for instance, are interrupted more frequently than men.

Being intentional about who gets to speak and how their contributions are acknowledged can reshape power dynamics in subtle but meaningful ways.

## Cultural Perspectives on Workplace Communication

In today's global and multicultural workplaces, understanding the cultural lens through which communication is filtered is essential. Different cultures bring different expectations and styles. In high-context cultures like Japan or China, communication is often indirect and relies heavily on shared understanding, body language, and relationship dynamics.

What's not said can be just as important as what is. In contrast, low-context cultures such as the U.S. or Germany prioritize directness and clarity—messages are typically straightforward and leave little room for interpretation. These differences show up especially in how feedback is delivered. For example, a manager from a high-context culture might gently suggest improvements through hints, while a low-context manager may offer blunt, honest critique.

Recognizing these variations helps reduce misunderstandings, foster respect, and build a workplace that is both inclusive and globally competent.

**The Rise of AI and Automation in the Workplace**
The modern workplace is being reshaped by a wave of artificial intelligence and automation tools that are changing not only how we communicate, but also how we understand connection itself. From chatbots that answer customer questions in milliseconds to virtual assistants that help manage schedules and AI-powered tools that draft emails or filter resumes, these technologies promise speed and efficiency like never before.

And while there's no denying the time-saving benefits, these innovations also raise important questions. Are we sacrificing human connection for convenience? Can automated messaging ever replace the value of thoughtful, face-to-face conversation?

One of the most pressing challenges is the balance between efficiency and personalization. For example, an automated email can quickly distribute information across a company, but it rarely conveys empathy, nuance, or sincerity.

When trust and workplace morale are on the line, a generic message can feel impersonal—or even dismissive. As a result, leaders and team members alike must think critically about when to automate and when to engage more personally.

There's also growing concern about bias embedded in AI systems. These technologies are only as fair as the data they're trained on, and if that data reflects existing societal biases, those same disparities can be amplified in workplace communication.

Take, for example, AI-driven applicant tracking systems. These tools are used to screen resumes before a human ever sees them. But if the algorithms favor certain schools, experiences, or language patterns, qualified candidates can be overlooked—often without anyone realizing why.

Remote and hybrid work environments add another layer of complexity. Digital communication tools are the lifeline for distributed teams, but they come with their own set of expectations and etiquette. How do we build cohesion across time zones? How do we ensure that asynchronous communication doesn't create feelings of isolation or disconnect?

In an era where emoji reactions can replace water cooler conversations, organizations must be intentional about cultivating human connection in the digital space.

**The Power of Effective Workplace Communication**
At its core, workplace communication is not just about sharing information—it's about connection, trust, and influence. The most successful professionals aren't necessarily the loudest or the most charismatic, but the ones who know how to express themselves clearly, listen actively, and tailor their message to different contexts and audiences.

Strong communication inspires action, fosters collaboration, and helps build resilient teams, especially during times of change or uncertainty.

Great communicators don't just speak. They also pay attention. They recognize when a colleague needs encouragement, when a conversation needs reframing, or when silence says more than words ever could.

These are the people who shape team culture, build bridges across departments, and become the kind of leaders others want to follow.

As we continue exploring communication in complex, fast-paced environments, we begin to see that communication is not just a professional skill—it's a human one.

## The Life Cycle of Connection

As we have seen in the preceding chapters, relationships are not static—they evolve, stretch, deepen, or sometimes fade. Whether with coworkers, family, friends, or romantic partners, our connections shape how we see ourselves and the world around us.

What makes a relationship meaningful isn't just compatibility or shared history—it's the day-to-day choices we make to nurture, challenge, and sustain it.

Knowing what makes relationships work is just the beginning. The true test comes in tending—showing up when it's uncomfortable, setting boundaries when needed, and learning to recognize when to hold on and when to let go.

How do we keep connections alive through conflict? How do we stay present with one another in a world full of distractions? What do we do when something once beautiful begins to shift or dissolve?

This section marks a turning point in our journey. If the earlier chapters gave us a glimpse of the roots of human connection, what comes next invites us into the garden itself.

Relationships, like gardens, do not flourish on intention alone. They require pruning, patience, presence, and sometimes, the courage to replant in new soil. In the chapters ahead, we'll step into that messy, tender middle—where conflict meets compassion, where boundaries coexist with vulnerability, and where the lifelong art of communication truly comes to life.

## *Chapter Nine Reflection Questions*

1. Think about a time when you had to navigate a difficult conversation at work. How did your tone, timing, or delivery impact the outcome?
2. Reflect on the leadership styles of people you've worked with in the past. Who inspired you most—and why?
3. Have you ever felt overlooked or misunderstood in a professional setting because of the way someone else communicated with you? How did you respond, and what might you do differently now?
4. How has remote/hybrid work changed the way you connect with coworkers? What tools or habits have helped you stay engaged and build trust from distance?
5. In what ways can you use your current role—regardless of title—to help create a more inclusive and equitable communication culture in your workplace?
6. Consider a time when feedback—positive or negative—had a lasting effect on you. What made the delivery of that feedback effective or ineffective?
7. How do you typically respond to power dynamics in communication (e.g., speaking to a supervisor versus a peer)? What patterns have you noticed in yourself?
8. Have you ever unintentionally communicated in a way that was passive-aggressive, dismissive, or unclear? What was the impact, and what did you learn?
9. What communication habits or traits do you admire most in great leaders like Ted Lasso, Indra Nooyi, or Oprah Winfrey? How can you embody some of those in your own interactions?
10. Reflect on how cultural communication differences have shown up in your past work or school experiences. What surprised you, challenged you, or helped you grow?

## *Chapter Nine Challenges*

1. This week, observe the communication styles of your teammates during meetings. Can you identify at least one assertive, passive, aggressive, or passive-aggressive behavior? Write down your observations and reflect on how those styles affected the discussion.
2. Choose one piece of feedback you need to give or receive this week. Use the SBI method (Situation, Behavior, Impact) to prepare or interpret the message. Note how it changes clarity/tone of the conversation.
3. Audit your own communication. Review a recent email or message you sent to a team or supervisor. Did it reflect clarity, empathy, and intentionality? Revise it as if you were sending it today, incorporating emotionally intelligent language.
4. Try leading a small group discussion or meeting with one leadership trait in mind—whether it's emotional intelligence, active listening, or adaptability. Then, jot down how the group responded.
5. Practice speaking up in a situation where you might typically stay silent. Notice how it feels to take up space assertively.
6. Pay attention to your use of inclusive language over the next few days. Replace any gendered or exclusive phrases ("you guys," "manpower," "crazy") with neutral, respectful alternatives.
7. If you're in a hybrid or remote environment, experiment with one way to humanize your digital communication—like sending a thoughtful Slack message, voice note, or handwritten thank-you.
8. Explore a new communication platform or AI tool used in the workplace. Reflect on how it helps or hinders authentic human connection. Would you recommend it to your team?

# PART 3:

# TENDING YOUR RELATIONSHIP GARDEN

## Nurturing Connection Through Conflict, Boundaries, and Renewal

*"To plant a garden is to believe in tomorrow."*
— Audrey Hepburn

Every relationship is a living thing, much like a garden. Some are wild and spontaneous—like vines that reach for whatever light they can find. Others are delicate and need protection, blooming only in safe and intentional spaces. Some grow deep roots slowly over time; others burst into being like spring wildflowers—bright, brief, and breathtaking.

But no matter their shape or season, **all relationships require care**. They require attention. And they require the wisdom to know when to water, when to prune, and when to let something go.

This section invites you into the work of relational gardening. You are not just observing your relationships—you're tending them. That means stepping into discomfort when conflict arises. It means clearing out the weeds of assumption and silence. It means building trellises of trust through boundaries that support—not stifle—connection. And yes, it means grieving the relationships that no longer have space to bloom.

We're not aiming for perfection. We're aiming for presence. We are aiming for the kind of emotional honesty that strengthens our roots, even when the weather turns.

The truth is that whether it's your garden, your muscles, or your relationships, **growth is not always graceful.** But it is always possible.

### Chapter 10: *When Communication Breaks Down*
We begin by digging into the tangled roots of misunderstanding—why conflict happens even in loving relationships, and how early weeds of miscommunication can become overgrowth if left unchecked. This chapter offers tools for repair, empathy, and restoring clarity before assumptions take over.

### Chapter 11: *Strengthening Relationships Through Emotional Intelligence and Boundaries*
Here, we learn to build the trellis. Emotional intelligence becomes the nutrient-rich soil, and boundaries provide structure and protection. This chapter explores how to love without losing yourself, how to hold space for others without abandoning your own needs, and how culture, upbringing, and identity shape the way we set (or avoid) limits.

## Chapter 12: *From Tending to Thriving: The Art of Relationship Maintenance*

We move from repair and structure into daily tending—how consistency, reciprocity, and adaptability form the rhythm of lasting connection. It's not grand gestures that sustain relationships, but the small acts of care, repeated. This chapter invites you to consider what kind of presence you offer, and how to keep your relationships alive through change.

## Chapter 13: *When Something Ends*

Finally, we reach the part of the garden most people fear: the ending. But letting go isn't failure—it's a form of wisdom. This chapter walks with you through grief, ambiguity, identity shifts, and emotional composting—transforming what's been lost into something nourishing for your next chapter.

Some relationships will stay with us for a lifetime. Others will pass through, leaving pollen behind—something invisible but transformative. Through it all, we get to choose: to show up, weed and water, trim and tend.

Let this section be a greenhouse: a place to experiment, reflect, and grow. Rather than becoming a perfect gardener, aim to be a present one. Be fully engaged in your relationships, committed to their growth and health.

Let's begin!

# WE RELATE

# Chapter 10:

# When Communication Breaks Down

*"Peace is not the absence of conflict, but the ability to handle conflict by peaceful means."*
— Ronald Reagan

**Clearing Weeds, Misunderstandings, Conflict, and the Opportunity to Repair**
In any thriving garden, weeds will inevitably appear. Some are tiny misunderstandings that take root in the quiet spaces between words. Others are more significant, overgrown, and thorny conflicts that can choke out even the strongest connections if left untended. And just like in gardening, ignoring the problem will make it harder to pull up later.

**Why do even loving relationships experience conflict?**
Conflict is a sign that something needs attention, but many of us fear conflict because we don't know how to face it without hurting others or losing ourselves. Our brains fill in the blanks of unclear communication with assumptions, usually negative ones. A late reply becomes a rejection. A sarcastic comment feels like a personal attack. A quiet moment turns into a perceived emotional storm.

This chapter is a guide to recognizing the weeds early, approaching conflict not as a threat but as a chance to *rebuild trust*, and making room for more profound understanding through clear, compassionate communication. It's a journey of growth and learning, offering hope and motivation for those seeking to improve their relationships. Change is possible, and it starts with you.

## The Ripple Effect of Miscommunication

Think back to the iconic *"We were on a break"* moment between Ross and Rachel in *Friends*. A single phrase, interpreted differently by each person, led to seasons of emotional fallout. Or consider the comedic chaos in *The Office*, where tone-deaf jokes and passive-aggressive silence turn office friendships into landmines. Even *Pride and Prejudice*, a literature classic, shows how pride, assumptions, and misread intentions can nearly ruin a powerful connection.

These are just a few examples of how miscommunication and conflict can manifest in different relationships and settings. For instance, a misunderstanding between a boss and an employee, a miscommunication between friends, or a conflict between family members can significantly impact the relationships involved.

Miscommunication is not just a modern problem. It is a universal human experience that happens to us all, regardless of the relationship or setting. Emphasizing the universal nature of miscommunication helps the reader feel less isolated in their struggles and more open to learning and growth.

Trey once sent an email that he believed was clear and professional. The recipient read it as cold and condescending. Rather than seeking clarity, they withdrew. They finally talked weeks later and realized they'd both been operating from misinterpretations.

A single conversation could have saved them from weeks of tension—if only they'd been willing to uproot the weed early. This experience teaches the importance of clear communication and the potential consequences of relationship misinterpretation. Similarly, you might recall a time when a miscommunication led to a conflict in your own life. Reflecting on these experiences can help you understand the concepts discussed in this chapter.

**Think About It:** Have you ever misread someone's words? Or have you ever felt misread yourself? These experiences are powerful tools for learning and growth in your relationships. Take a moment to reflect on them and see how you can use them to your advantage.

## When Meaning Gets Lost in the Weeds

Think back to a time when a conversation went sideways. Maybe it was a text that sounded colder than intended, or a joke that didn't land. What might have shifted if you had paused to ask for clarity rather than reacting? Even when we care deeply, the words we speak and the ways they're received don't always align. That's because healthy communication requires more than good intentions—it requires awareness, empathy, and a willingness to navigate the invisible forces shaping our interpretations.

Psychologists point to several internal biases that affect how we receive messages. One of the biggest culprits is **negativity bias**—our brain's tendency to focus on perceived threats. This survival instinct means we're more likely to read a neutral message ("We need to talk") as a warning siren rather than a simple request.

**Confirmation bias** adds another twist, leading us to interpret ambiguous words through the lens of our past wounds. If you've felt dismissed or ignored in past relationships, even a short delay in response might feel like rejection.

And then there's **emotional contagion**—how one person's anxiety or frustration can subconsciously ripple through a conversation like an unexpected frost in an otherwise healthy garden.

Pop culture reminds us of this all the time. In *This Is Us*, we see how generational trauma and unspoken fears create a web of misunderstanding between family members. Even in *Euphoria*, Rue and Jules' relationship is complicated by unspoken expectations and unhealed pain, showing how communication—or the lack of it—can either strengthen or erode trust.

### Identity Shapes the Way We Speak and Hear

Just like a gardener brings their unique tools, seeds, and soil to their planting, every person brings a unique identity to how they communicate. Gender norms play a major role—some people are raised to express their emotions freely, while others are conditioned to bottle them up. Cultural background also influences style. For example, in the U.S. and Germany, directness is often valued and even equated with honesty. But in cultures like Japan or India, harmony and indirect expression may take priority, and being too blunt can be seen as disrespectful.

### We Bring Our Whole Selves Into Every Conversation

We don't enter relationships as blank slates—we bring our full selves: our upbringing, race, gender, values, generational influences, and faith traditions. This is what scholar Kimberlé Crenshaw calls intersectionality—the idea that multiple identities intersect to shape how we experience the world, including how we give and receive love.

In *Crazy Rich Asians*, Rachel and Nick's relationship isn't threatened by lack of love, but by the collision of cultural expectations and familial duty. Similarly, in *Modern Family*, we see how identity—age, gender, sexuality, culture—shapes the way characters approach (and often fumble) communication. These stories echo our own experiences: that we're all tending to different kinds of gardens, with different tools, in different seasons. What looks like a weed to one person might be a wildflower to another.

Faith and worldview add another layer. Spiritual or moral beliefs often shape how we apologize, how we view conflict, and whether we believe silence is sacred or suffocating. These roots grow deep, and if we're not aware of them, we may misinterpret each other's actions through our own limited lens. As sociolinguist Deborah Tannen noted in her research, even small differences in conversational style can lead to major misunderstandings if we're not paying attention to what lies beneath the surface.

## The Psychology of Misunderstanding

At the core of many communication breakdowns is the mind's attempt to protect itself. When someone doesn't text back, when a conversation feels curt, when silence stretches longer than expected—our minds often fill in the blanks. And they rarely fill them in kindly. What's meant as "I need a minute" may be received as "I don't care." In the digital world, this becomes even more complicated. Without tone, body language, or eye contact, we are left to decode intent with limited tools.

Like a gardener mistaking shade for drought, we often misread our partner's silence as rejection or interpret brevity as disinterest. But when we slow down, ask questions, and choose curiosity over assumption, we give ourselves the chance to water something meaningful instead of pulling it out by the roots.

## Misreading the Soil

Trey once dated someone who grew up in a culture that deeply valued emotional restraint and avoiding conflict for the sake of peace. For her, speaking directly about disagreements felt disrespectful. Trey, on the other hand, came from a background that encouraged open dialogue and direct honesty. He saw clarity as a way to build trust—she experienced it as confrontation. They weren't wrong for feeling the way they did—but they kept misreading the soil they were trying to grow something in. Without understanding each other's communication roots, even the most heartfelt conversations became tangled.

**Tending the Garden: Navigating Conflict with Care**
Conflict doesn't mean something is broken—it means something matters. Like pulling weeds from a garden, navigating conflict takes intention and care. The first step is to name the issue early. Tiny miscommunications, if left unattended, often take root and grow into major misunderstandings. Next, choose to respond, not react. Emotional regulation is key—because when our nervous system is in fight-or-flight, our ability to listen and empathize plummets.

Take breaks when things get too heated—not to storm off, but to reset. Agree ahead of time that time-outs are okay and will be followed up with return conversations. Use "I" statements to express your feelings without blame. Saying, "I feel hurt when you don't check in" lands differently than, "You never care."

And most importantly, listen to understand, not just to defend. Ask follow-up questions. Make space for discomfort.

When harm has been done, apologize well. A genuine apology names the impact, expresses remorse, and shows willingness to repair—not just a passive, "I'm sorry you feel that way."

And if you've tried all these things and the relationship still causes harm or imbalance, give yourself permission to step back or let go. Not all gardens are meant to grow forever—but that doesn't mean they didn't serve a season of beauty and growth.

**Think About It:** Have you ever apologized just to end a conflict rather than to repair it? What might a more sincere apology have sounded like?

## When to Walk Away: Knowing When to Replant
Some conflicts reveal deeper truths—like soil no longer fertile or a plant that can't thrive no matter how much you tend to it. If the pattern is one of disrespect, manipulation, or emotional harm, the healthiest choice may be to uproot and make space for something better.

### When the Garden Begins to Wither
Not every difficult conversation is a red flag—but when patterns begin to repeat without repair, it's time to take a closer look. Communication breakdowns can be subtle at first, like a creeping vine in an otherwise healthy garden. But if left unchecked, they can choke out trust, connection, and emotional safety.

You might be in a communication dynamic that's out of balance if you constantly feel misunderstood, yet you're the one repeatedly blamed for the conflict. Over time, this pattern can lead to emotional exhaustion, especially if efforts to repair or improve the relationship are one-sided. A healthy relationship requires two people who are both willing to weed, water, and grow. If only one person keeps showing up with tools in hand, something's off.

Another major red flag is when apologies are weaponized or avoided—not as a genuine expression of remorse but as a deflection tool to shift guilt or silence accountability. As clinical psychologist Dr. Harriet Lerner puts it, "A true apology does not include the word 'but.'" When communication becomes a battleground of blame instead of a bridge to better understanding, it's a sign the soil needs tending—or replanting altogether.

These dynamics are reflected across pop culture, too. In the Netflix series *You*, Joe's charming exterior hides a deeply manipulative communication style, with him apologizing only to regain control, not to make amends. In *The Notebook*, we see the volatility of Noah and Allie's connection, romanticized for its passion, yet deeply rooted in patterns of miscommunication and reactive emotion. These stories remind us that intensity is not the same as intimacy, and, without healthy communication, love alone is not enough to sustain growth.

**Clearing the Weeds: Reflecting with Compassion**
Like any living thing, relationships require routine tending. That doesn't mean conflict is bad—in fact, conflict can be a powerful sign that something wants to grow.

But before we get there, we have to examine our own tools. What conversations are you avoiding because they feel too complex or emotionally charged? Are you holding onto assumptions about what someone *meant* rather than clarifying what they actually said?

Our identity plays a significant role in how we approach these moments. Maybe your upbringing taught you to avoid conflict at all costs, or perhaps you come from a culture that values indirect communication and reading between the lines. Understanding your communication roots helps you grow with more intention.

**Try this in real life**: Next time you receive a message that makes your chest tighten or your heart race, don't respond immediately. Take a breath. Try saying, "Hey, I want to make sure I understand what you meant. can we talk about it?" That one sentence can open the door to clarity rather than closing it with assumptions. And don't underestimate the power of journaling.

Reflect on a time when conflict *strengthened* a relationship rather than breaking it. What allowed that growth?

**Conflict Is a Sign That Something Wants to Grow**
Too often, we treat conflict as a sign of failure. But conflict is not the enemy of connection—it's a symptom of something deeper stirring. A weed in the garden isn't a threat if it's caught early and pulled with care. Sometimes, it's even a sign that something valuable is nearby—something worth protecting, redefining, or replanting.

Research supports this. According to Drs. John and Julie Gottman, it's not whether couples fight, but *how* they fight that determines the long-term success of their relationship. The most resilient couples and friendships aren't the ones who avoid conflict—they're the ones who repair after it. They make space for tension without turning away. They listen with curiosity instead of defensiveness.

In pop culture, we see this kind of redemptive conflict in shows like *Ted Lasso*, where difficult conversations aren't glossed over—they're embraced with vulnerability and trust. Ted doesn't avoid tough conversations with his team or friends. He leans in, listens fully, and uses emotional intelligence as a tool for healing and growth. That's the work of real connection.

So the next time a relationship hits a rough patch, remember: some gardens just need a little weeding, a bit more sunlight, and the water of honest conversation to bloom again.

## *Chapter Ten Reflection Questions*

1. Think of a recent miscommunication—what assumptions did you make before seeking clarity?
2. When conflict arises, do you tend to avoid it, confront it directly, or seek harmony at your own expense? Where do you think that pattern comes from?
3. Which of the cognitive biases mentioned (negativity bias, confirmation bias, emotional contagion) do you recognize most in yourself?
4. What role does your upbringing or cultural background play in how you express disagreement or handle tough conversations?
5. Reflect on a time when conflict actually strengthened a relationship. What made that possible?
6. Who in your life models healthy conflict resolution? What do they do that stands out to you?
7. Have you ever stayed in a relationship that consistently drained you emotionally?
8. How do you typically feel after a conflict—relieved, regretful, exhausted, empowered? What does that say about your current communication habits?

## *Chapter Ten Challenges*

1. Conflict Journal: Over the next week, write down every conflict—big or small—that you experience. What was said, what wasn't, and how did you respond? Reflect on any recurring patterns.
2. Rewrite the Story: Take a past conflict and rewrite it with a healthier communication script. Replace blame with "I" statements, add curiosity, and imagine a different ending.
3. Practice the Pause: The next time you receive a message that stings, don't respond right away. Instead, wait 20 minutes. Journal your initial reaction, then respond with emotional clarity and empathy.
4. Repair Attempt: Revisit a strained relationship where miscommunication led to distance. Try reaching out with an honest, kind message seeking understanding—not blame.
5. Media Reflection: Watch a favorite show (*Ted Lasso*, *This Is Us*, *Modern Family*, etc.) and write a reflection on how a character handles conflict. What could they have done differently?
6. Bias Awareness Day: For one day, pay attention to your internal assumptions during every conversation. Note how often your thoughts jump to the worst-case scenario or past wounds.
7. Cultural Insight: Interview a friend or peer from a different cultural background about how conflict is handled in their family or culture. Reflect on what you learned and how it compares to your own experience.

# WE RELATE

# Chapter 11:

# Strengthening Relationships Through Emotional Intelligence and Boundaries

"Daring to set boundaries is about having the courage to love ourselves, even when we risk disappointing others."
- Brené Brown

### Building the Trellis: Structure, Safety, and the Space to Grow

If communication is the sunlight that helps relationships grow, then boundaries are the trellises and fences—the supportive structures that give relationships their shape, clarity, and direction. Much like in a garden, without these forms of gentle guidance, even the most beautiful connection can sprawl out uncontrollably, choking other areas of life, sapping energy, and leaving emotional burnout in its wake.

### *How do we build strong relationships without losing ourselves in the process?*

What begins as closeness can quickly become entanglement. And the worst part? It often happens gradually, without either person realizing it—until one of them can't breathe.

Strong boundaries don't weaken connection; they protect it. They make relationships sustainable by preserving energy, identity, and mutual respect. But in many homes, communities, and cultures, we're not taught how to set or receive boundaries well.

Instead, we're conditioned to believe that setting limits makes us selfish, cold, or even disloyal. This is especially true for women, people of color, and those raised in collectivist or faith-centered environments where "sacrifice" is often equated with love.

But boundaries are not walls built to push people away. They're containers—clear, intentional structures that hold space for honest growth, emotional safety, and reciprocity. They are the blueprint for building healthy, life-giving connections that endure across seasons of change.

This chapter explores how emotional intelligence (EQ)—the nutrient-rich soil beneath our communication—enables us to understand and express our needs with compassion and clarity. When EQ is high, boundaries are no longer threatening. They become invitations: to be fully known, deeply respected, and safely loved.

### The Cost of Boundary Avoidance

Perhaps you identify with being a person who isn't great at saying no. The one who stays late at work taking on extra tasks even when they are already feeling behind, answers calls from friends who never asked how you are doing, and accommodates partners who require emotional caretaking but offer little in return.

If you can relate with this, you understand how every unspoken "no" disguised as a "yes" can begin to feel like a piece of your peace is evaporating. You can become overextended and burnt out. This type of boundary erosion can feel like a withering of your garden, not from neglect of others, but from self-neglect. This leads to exhaustion, disconnection, and breeds resentment.

According to therapist and researcher Dr. Thema Bryant, people who struggle with boundaries often have a deep history of over-functioning—a coping response developed from trauma, people-pleasing, or cultural norms that discourage self-prioritization. The result? Emotional burnout masked as busyness, resentment masked as helpfulness.

As bestselling author Prentis Hemphill puts it, *"Boundaries are the distance at which I can love you and me simultaneously."*

**Think About It:** Have you ever felt guilty for setting a boundary or exhausted because you didn't? What would it feel like to put your own emotional needs in the soil first?

### Learning Emotional Intelligence

Psychologist Daniel Goleman popularized the term emotional intelligence, or EQ, to describe the ability to recognize, understand, and manage our emotions—and to do the same for others. High EQ doesn't mean you're always calm or agreeable. It means you have the tools to respond instead of react. It means you're aware of what's happening inside of you and curious about what's happening inside of others.

Goleman outlined four foundational components of EQ:

1. **Self-Awareness** – Recognizing your emotions and understanding how they influence your behavior.
2. **Self-Regulation** – Managing emotional impulses before they hijack your actions.
3. **Empathy** – Understanding and caring about others' emotional experiences.
4. **Relationship Management** – Navigating conflict, building trust, and fostering clear communication.

In relationships, EQ helps us **tend to our garden** without trampling someone else's roots. It creates space for honesty without cruelty, vulnerability without chaos, and disagreement without destruction.

**Think About It:** Where does emotional intelligence show up most in your life— friendships, classes, family, or work? Where does it disappear when you need it most?

### Why We Struggle With Boundaries

Even the most emotionally intelligent people struggle with setting boundaries. That's because boundary resistance is often wired into us—from our families, cultures, religions, or past relationships. Boundaries feel hard because they disrupt patterns. But disruption can be healthy. It's how we prune the branches so something better can grow.

Some of us were raised to believe that love means self-sacrifice. Others were conditioned to fear rejection or abandonment if we dared to say "no."

Cultural narratives often paint boundary-setters as cold or confrontational, especially for women and marginalized groups. Cultural conditioning, gender roles, and lived experience shape whether we feel free to say "no" or compelled to say "yes" out of guilt, fear, or duty. People-pleasing often sounds like, "If I set a boundary, they'll think I'm selfish." Fear of abandonment whispers, "If I say no, they'll leave." Guilt chimes in with, "I owe them my time, even if I'm running on empty."

Dr. Nedra Glover Tawwab, author of *Set Boundaries, Find Peace*, explains that when we don't set limits, we unconsciously teach others that we're always available—at the expense of our own peace.

**The Global Garden: Boundaries Around the World**
Just as every garden thrives in a specific climate, boundaries are shaped by cultural context. In many Western cultures, direct and verbal boundary-setting is encouraged—people are taught to speak up and be assertive. Saying, "I need space" is seen as healthy self-care.

But in collectivist cultures like Japan, India, and parts of Latin America, emotional needs are often communicated indirectly, in ways that prioritize group harmony over personal assertion. There, boundaries are often communicated through subtlety, body language, or indirect language.

Neither approach is superior. They simply reflect different values—autonomy versus community, clarity versus preservation. Understanding these nuances allows us to practice compassion over frustration. When a friend hesitates to say "no," it may not be avoidance—it may be an act of respect according to their cultural lens.

Pop culture reflects this tension. In *Crazy Rich Asians*, Rachel's assertive, Western communication style clashes with Nick's family's more indirect and traditional values. The resulting conflict isn't about right or wrong—it's about differing boundary languages. In *Everything Everywhere All At Once*, we witness a complex mother-daughter dynamic where love, duty, and identity all collide. These stories show us the nuanced reality: that sometimes, the hardest boundaries to set are with the people we love most.

**Boundaries Are a Form of Love—Not Rejection**

Let's reframe boundaries. They're not about shutting people out—they're about showing up with your whole self. Healthy boundaries don't shut people out—they invite them in **with clarity and care**. They tell others how we wish to be loved and respected. They protect not just our peace, but the relationship itself. Consider the different forms a boundary might take:

- **Emotional:**
  *"I need space after arguments before we talk again."*
  *"I'm happy to support you, but I can't be your only source of emotional care."*

- **Time-Based:**
  *"I'm not available after 9 p.m. unless it's urgent."*
  *"I can't text during work hours, but I'll respond later tonight."*

- **Physical:**
  *"I'm okay with hugs, but only when I initiate them."*
  *"Please ask before touching my stuff, even if we're roommates."*

- **Mental:**
  *"I respect your beliefs, but I see things differently—and that's okay."*
  *"I'm open to discussion, but I'm not okay with being mocked or dismissed."*

- **Academic/Professional:**
  *"I can't take on your part of the group project—I need us both to contribute."*
  *"I need a quiet space to focus. Can we catch up after I finish this assignment?"*
- **Relational/Personal Time:**
  *"I love spending time with you, but I also need alone time to recharge."*
  *"I'm not ready to label this relationship yet, and I need you to respect that."*

Boundaries are not rigid rules. They are invitations to **mutual respect**, where both people feel safe enough to be honest and whole. Boundaries create containers for trust to grow—spaces where we can be ourselves without apology and still remain connected.

Just like a garden doesn't thrive when overrun with vines or weeds, relationships can't flourish without structure. Some plants need a trellis, some need a fence, and some simply need space. Key is knowing what your garden—and your heart—needs to grow strong, not just survive.

**Think About It:** What would change in your closest relationship if you communicated your needs more clearly—and kindly? Would you gain peace, risk tension, or maybe both?

### Pop Culture and Boundary Breakdowns

TV and film offer us rich metaphors for how boundaries and emotional intelligence shape relationships. *Ted Lasso* shows us what it looks like to lead with empathy and emotional insight, even when conflict arises. Ted gives his players space to grow, guiding them like a well-placed trellis rather than a suffocating vine. Ted doesn't dominate his team—he listens, adapts, and models vulnerability. His leadership is rooted in emotional safety.

In contrast, *Succession* offers a warning. Logan Roy may have wealth and authority, but his absence of empathy breeds a toxic culture. His children constantly betray and belittle each other, all desperate for connection in a family that doesn't know how to nurture.

These examples remind us that **emotional intelligence turns authority into leadership**—and boundaries turn chaos into connection.

## Cross-Cultural Insight: Different Gardens, Different Tools

Whether you grew up in a faith-based family that prized duty over dialogue, or a household where silence was mistaken for strength, you bring your own toolkit into every interaction. And so does everyone else. The more we **honor our differences**—not just in culture but in gender, identity, neurodiversity, and values—the more generous and flexible we become in the ways we love.

### The Takeaway

When we avoid boundaries, we don't just damage our relationships—we abandon ourselves. And when we honor boundaries, we don't end relationships—we give them a chance to thrive in healthier soil.

If Emotional Intelligence is the soil, then boundaries are the trellis—the structure that helps love and connection grow upward instead of sprawling out and taking over every inch of space. Together, they allow us to love without losing ourselves—and to be loved without being consumed.

Boundaries don't block love. Instead, they serve to protect it. They allow connection to grow within a space that's safe, respectful, and sustainable.

So maybe the question isn't: "What if they leave when I set a boundary?" Maybe the better question is: "What if I finally come home to myself?"

## *Chapter Eleven Reflection Questions*

1. What's a "yes" I've given recently that I *secretly* wanted to be a "no"?
   What stopped me from being honest in that moment, and what was the impact?
2. How do I usually respond when someone sets a boundary with *me*?
   Do I get defensive, grateful, indifferent, confused? What might that say about how I was raised to view boundaries?
3. If I could design a "relational trellis" for my life right now, what would it look like?
   What structures, routines, or boundaries would help me grow without getting tangled?
4. How have I confused "being nice" with "being available at all costs"? How has that affected my energy, identity, or relationships?
5. Which emotional habits have I inherited from my family—and do they still serve me today?
   For example, do I bottle things up? Do I over-apologize? Do I retreat instead of resolving?
6. What's a boundary I admire in someone else? How do they model strength *without* being harsh?
7. How have I used humor, distraction, or overachievement to avoid setting boundaries?
   What might happen if I dropped the performance and just said what I need?
8. What's one loving boundary I wish someone had taught me earlier in life? How would that have changed the way I communicate today?

## *Chapter Eleven Challenges*

1. Boundary Role Reversal Ask a trusted friend or roommate to set a boundary with you—real or hypothetical. Practice receiving it without defensiveness. Then switch. Reflect together on how it felt.
2. The "Pre-Burnout" Radar Check. Write down 3 signals that typically show up *before* you burn out emotionally (e.g., snapping at people, ghosting texts, binge-watching for 8 hours straight). Pick one and choose a boundary that could help intercept it.
3. DM Detox (Boundary with Your Phone). For one full day, set a boundary with your tech: no responding to messages for 3 hours during peak social media scroll time. Journal about what that space created—or what came up in the quiet.
4. EQ in the Wild. Choose a group project, club meeting, or dorm conversation this week and make it your personal "EQ Lab."
   Practice:
   - Naming your emotions (to yourself).
   - Asking someone how they *feel* about something, not just what they think.
   - Taking a pause before reacting to something that annoys you.
     Then, rate your performance honestly. No shame, just growth.
5. Redraw the Map. Pick a relationship where the emotional "map" feels unclear or draining. Write a short script of how you could clarify your needs or expectations in a kind, direct way. Bonus: If it feels safe, try using it.

# WE RELATE

# Chapter 12:

# From Tending to Thriving: The Art of Relationship Maintenance

*"Love is not about grand intentions, but about small actions repeated daily."*
　　　　　— *Esther Perel*

### Daily Watering: Nurturing Connection Through Consistency and Change

We talk a lot about the beginning of relationships—first impressions, first texts, first kisses, first DMs that lead to long walks that lead to inside jokes. And we talk about the end—breakups, ghosting, the silence that slowly replaces what used to be everything. But what about the middle?

What about the stretch in between—the part where you've chosen someone, or they've chosen you, and now you're trying to figure out how to stay connected while life keeps shifting around you?

This is the real work of relationship: **maintenance**. Not sexy. Not trending. But absolutely essential.

Ask any long-distance best friend, any college student balancing new freedom and old loyalties, any young couple figuring out how to communicate without spiraling, and they'll tell you: it's not just the deep talks that keep you close. It's the shared memes. The birthday reminders. The small check-ins. The way you remember their Thursday morning class is brutal and send a "you got this" voice note just because.

Every relationship starts with excitement. But the ones that last? They're the ones where someone kept showing up after the excitement faded.

Trey learned this the hard way. After college, the friend group that once felt inseparable started to dissolve. Not out of drama, but out of silence. Out of life. Jobs. Distance. New partners. New cities. He kept waiting for someone to check in until he realized: maybe they were waiting, too. So he started watering the garden. Voice notes. Spontaneous Facetimes. Birthday texts that said more than "HBD." Most friendships perked back up with little effort. Others not so much. Either way, it feels good to show people you are thinking of them, that you care.

That's what this chapter is about. Choosing to care about people because relationships don't run on autopilot. They run on intention.

## The Anatomy of Daily Tending

There's a scene early on in *Ted Lasso*—before anyone fully trusts him, before the team believes in his vision—where he walks into the office with a small pink box of biscuits. He doesn't make a big deal of it. He just sets it down, smiles, and says something like, "Morning. How's your day looking?" The biscuits keep coming, day after day, even when they're met with sarcasm or suspicion.

Eventually, the gesture softens something. Not because it's flashy, but because it's consistent. That's what daily tending looks like.

People may often assume relationships are built in big moments—confessions, crises, grand gestures. And yes, those matter. But most of the emotional infrastructure of our relationships is made of much smaller things: the text that says "Thinking of you." The friend who remembers your exam date. The roommate who leaves the hallway light on when you're out late. It's not that any of these gestures are the relationship. It's that they reveal something deeper: I see you. I know you. I care.

In the relationships that last—not just in length, but in depth—there's a rhythm underneath the surface. Not loud. Not constant. But steady. And that steadiness is usually composed of three key elements: consistency, reciprocity, and adaptability.

### Consistency: Showing Up With Intention

Consistency isn't about constant contact. It's about reliable presence. Emotionally consistent people are often the ones you feel safest with—not because they have all the right words, but because they don't vanish when things get hard.

In *Somebody Somewhere*, a tender series about grief, identity, and small-town life, we watch a friendship unfold between Sam and Joel—not through big moments, but through small ones. Texts. Singing sessions. Honest late-night conversations. The friendship doesn't hinge on drama; it grows through repetition. Their presence becomes the thing that heals.

Psychologist John Gottman calls this kind of interaction a "bid for connection." It can be as small as a shared joke, a casual "how was your day?" or a quick message with no agenda.

In decades of research on relationship longevity, Gottman found that thriving relationships tend to respond to these bids with attention and care. Not always perfectly—but consistently.

## Reciprocity: A Rhythm, Not a Scorecard
Healthy relationships don't require perfect balance—but they do require mutual investment. Not in a transactional way, but in the sense that both people are reaching for each other, even if in different ways.

Trey once told me about a friendship that felt one-sided. He was always the one initiating. Planning hangouts. Checking in. At first, he shrugged it off—"They're just busy," he'd say. But over time, that lopsided effort began to erode his trust in the connection. The truth wasn't that the other person didn't care—it's that they weren't showing it in a way that sustained the relationship.

Reciprocity doesn't mean doing the same thing at the same time. It means creating a shared sense of care. That might look like alternating who texts first. Or matching vulnerability when one person opens up. It might mean celebrating your friend's win even if your own week is falling apart. In *Heartstopper*, the quiet love story between Charlie and Nick reveals this beautifully. Their connection deepens not through perfection, but through mutual patience, curiosity, and care. One comes out. The other protects the space. They stretch toward each other—again and again.

If you want to take stock of a relationship's balance, ask yourself: When was the last time they checked in on me, unprompted? When was the last time I really listened to what they needed? The answers aren't meant to create guilt—they're meant to create clarity.

## Adaptability: Letting the Relationship Evolve
The final ingredient of sustainable connection is one we don't talk about enough: adaptability. People change. Lives shift. And if our relationships don't grow with us, they start to feel brittle—like we're holding onto a version of something that no longer fits.

In *Everything I Know About Love*, two best friends—once inseparable—find themselves growing in different directions. One gets into a relationship. The other leans into career exploration. What worked in their early twenties no longer holds. The tension isn't from betrayal—it's from transition. But instead of giving up, they begin to reimagine their friendship. They don't cling to the old rituals. They make room for new ones.

In real life, adaptability might look like shifting from weekly FaceTimes to monthly check-ins because your friend just had a baby. It might mean your dad stops giving unsolicited advice and starts simply asking, "How can I support you this week?" It might mean realizing that your closeness now looks different than it did before the move, the breakup, the new job.

Sometimes, people feel hurt when connection changes shape. But often, it's not that someone cares less—it's that they don't know how to care differently. This is where communication becomes a bridge. A simple, "I know things have changed, but I still want to feel close. Can we find a new rhythm?" can do more than a dozen silent assumptions ever could.

It's easy to assume people experience closeness the same way you do. But relational expectations are shaped by culture, upbringing, and lived experiences. In collectivist cultures, for example, connection may be tied to proximity and loyalty. Silence is not necessarily abandonment. It can signal respect, space, or emotional modesty.

In individualist cultures, meanwhile, connection is often linked to autonomy and shared interest. When life pulls people apart, the assumption might be: "If the bond matters, we'll naturally reconnect." Neither model is right or wrong. But when we forget that others bring different relational blueprints, we risk misreading their silence—or our own.

Culture can also shape how we interpret these shifts. In collectivist cultures, loyalty and proximity are often prioritized—even when life pulls people in new directions. In individualist cultures, space and self-focus are often expected during transitions. Knowing the expectations someone brings into a relationship—whether shaped by culture, personality, or past experiences—can help us navigate change with more empathy.

**Think About It:** Who in your life is showing up for you with quiet consistency? Whose efforts have you taken for granted? Is there a relationship that needs rebalancing—not because it's broken, but because it's out of rhythm? What version of a connection are you clinging to—when a new one is waiting to be formed?

## When Maintenance Turns Into Momentum

There's a kind of turning point in any relationship—romantic, platonic, professional, or familial—when the work of keeping it alive shifts into something softer, richer, more rewarding.

It's not that the effort disappears. But it begins to generate its own energy. What once required reminders or scheduling or self-talk—"I should reach out" or "We need to catch up"—becomes something you *want* to do. Something that fills you up instead of draining you.

That's when maintenance becomes momentum. In the early seasons of any connection, we invest heavily. We learn each other's stories. We show up with enthusiasm. We make time. But then life creeps in—work deadlines, emotional fatigue, physical distance—and the relationship either settles into autopilot or gets reenergized through intention. When it's the latter, something amazing happens: the daily tending starts to yield joy, depth, and even ease. The relationship doesn't feel like one more thing to manage—it feels like the thing that helps you manage everything else.

## The Science of Emotional Investment

Relationship researcher Caryl Rusbult once described this momentum as the "accumulation of commitment." In other words, every time we show up—respond to a bid for connection, forgive a mistake, or adjust during change—we add to the emotional capital of the relationship. Over time, that capital becomes a buffer. It allows us to weather conflict without unraveling. It sustains the relationship during dry spells. It creates a kind of safety net woven from trust, history, and shared meaning.

In *Reservation Dogs*, a show that blends humor, grief, and community with rare emotional honesty, we watch a group of teens trying to figure out who they are while navigating loss and transition. Their bond isn't smooth. They fight, flake out, and fumble through loyalty. But what keeps them connected isn't perfection—it's emotional capital. A thousand small moments of "I got you." Even when things get rocky, that foundation holds.

## From Rituals to Rhythms

Momentum often comes from shared rituals that turn into natural rhythms. Not everything has to be scheduled. Over time, your Monday night call with your sister becomes a given. Your Sunday morning texts with a friend become your version of church. Your check-in before a big test or job interview becomes a ritual of grounding—not because you planned it, but because it just *became*.

These rhythms don't have to be deep to be effective. A roommate who always brings you tea when you're studying. A partner who instinctively knows when to offer a hug without asking. A friend who sends the same meme every year on your "friendiversary." These are not distractions from the relationship—they *are* the relationship. They form the heartbeat of closeness.

Not all rituals are deep. Sometimes they're just weirdly delightful. One student told me about a college friend who texts them "don't combust" before every exam—no explanation, just a tradition now. Another friend group sends each other blurry selfies every Sunday night titled "Ghosts of the Weekend." It doesn't matter what it is—it matters that it's *yours*. Small, funny, oddly specific acts that say: "I'm here. I remember. We're still us."

## The Shift From "Effort" to "Energy"

Trey once described a friendship that started to feel different—not because it was easier, but because it was *energizing*. "I stopped asking myself if I was doing enough," he said. "Because I realized we'd created something where I could just be. And that was enough." That's the essence of momentum. When emotional safety has been built, maintenance stops being about checking a box and starts becoming a kind of emotional nutrition—something you're drawn to because it strengthens you.

But here's the thing: momentum is earned. It doesn't show up early. It doesn't come from hoping. It comes from tending. You can't skip the watering and expect the bloom.

## Momentum Isn't Always Mutual

Not every relationship will reach this phase. Some stay in maintenance forever. Others fade. And sometimes, people push for momentum in a relationship that's simply not designed to go there. It doesn't mean the connection was meaningless—it means its season might be shifting.

A former roommate you once texted daily might now live in a different rhythm. A college friend may move into a new phase of life that doesn't leave much room for the same depth of connection. That doesn't mean you stop caring. It just means you stop striving for a version of closeness that no longer fits.

This is where discernment becomes key. Ask yourself: Is this relationship feeding me back? Do I leave this interaction feeling more grounded, more seen, more real—or more anxious, more obligated, more invisible?

When the answer is the latter more often than not, it may be time for a different kind of tending: gentle release.

**Think About It:** What relationships in your life feel like they're gaining momentum—not just surviving, but enriching your days? Where do you feel more like a manager than a participant? What needs to shift for that to change? Which rituals in your relationships have naturally become rhythms? How did they start—and how might you deepen them now?

## How Thriving Relationships Sustain Us

Thriving isn't a static moment. It's not a finish line you cross or a badge you earn. It's more like the feeling you get when you walk into a room with someone and your shoulders drop just a little. When their name lighting up your phone feels like grounding instead of obligation. When you laugh so hard at an inside joke you almost forget the world outside.

That's full bloom.

It's what happens when a relationship has been tended, pruned, tested, and rooted deep enough to not just last—but feed your soul in return.

## What Thriving Feels Like

A graduate student once told me about her high school best friend. It was someone she hadn't lived near in years, hadn't gone to college with, and only saw in person once or twice a year. But they still thrived. Every time they reconnected, it felt seamless. She said, "It's like she reminds me who I am. I never have to explain myself. I just... arrive." That's the part of the magic of thriving relationships. They become places of return.

## The Four Pillars of Thriving
Psychologists and relational researchers consistently point to four key elements in sustaining meaningful, mutual connection over time. They aren't flashy. They're rarely cinematic. But they form the scaffolding of any relationship that doesn't just survive—but expands.

### 1. Trust and Reliability
This isn't about grand declarations. It's about following through on the small things. If you say you'll call—call. If you mess up—own it. Reliability builds safety. And safety is what allows people to be fully themselves.

In *Parks and Recreation*, the friendship between Leslie Knope and Ann Perkins works because of this. Leslie is chaotic and Ann is grounding. They're wildly different, but they always *show up*. Whether it's waffle brunches or job transitions or breakups, they're there—not always with the perfect words, but with presence. And over time, that consistency builds unshakable trust.

### 2. Emotional Intimacy
Thriving relationships make space for realness. You're not just talking logistics—you're talking *life*. Dreams. Doubts. Fears. Joy. The deep stuff. Emotional intimacy doesn't require constant vulnerability—but it does require honesty when it counts.

In *Modern Love*, one episode tells the story of a woman navigating bipolar disorder and her relationship with a man learning how to support her. They don't avoid the hard conversations. They step into them—awkwardly, bravely, imperfectly. That kind of emotional exposure is risky, but it's what allows love to be not just pretty—but powerful.

### 3. Mutual Growth
When one person evolves and the other resists, relationships strain. But when both people are committed

to becoming—not just to preserving who they've been—that's where thriving happens.

One young couple shared how they survived post-grad transitions by doing "monthly state-of-the-union" check-ins. No agendas, no performance—just honest reflection on how they're changing, what they're needing, and what they're hoping for. The check-ins didn't prevent every disagreement, but they created space to keep growing *with* each other, not apart.

### 4. Healthy Communication
Not constant. Not perfect. But honest, clear, and safe. In thriving relationships, misunderstandings don't fester. They get named. Needs aren't punished—they're welcomed. You learn to say things like:
- "I felt off when that happened—can we talk about it?"
- "I don't need advice, just presence right now."
- "Here's what support looks like for me—can we try that?"

In *The Marvelous Mrs. Maisel*, Midge's relationship with her manager, Susie, is a masterclass in messy but deep communication. They fight. They disappoint each other. But they also keep talking. And that talk? It keeps the relationship alive—even when everything else is changing.

### The Texture of Thriving
Thriving doesn't mean constant harmony. It means repair after rupture. It means rituals that remind you, "We're in this together." It means you get to be both deeply known *and* wildly encouraged to grow.

Sometimes it means making dinner together even though you're both tired. Other times it's calling out a friend gently when they're pulling away. Sometimes it's taking a break—and trusting that the bond is strong enough to hold.

And yes—thriving can fade if it's neglected. Like any garden, it still needs tending. But the difference is: once you've built that root system, it takes a lot more to shake it. Because you're not relying on good times to hold you together. You're relying on shared truth, chosen effort, and a deep knowing that this connection is worth it.

**Think About It:** Which relationship(s) in your life feel most like "full bloom"? What makes them feel that way? Which pillar—trust, emotional intimacy, growth, or communication—feels most alive in that relationship? Which one might need attention? What could you do this week to feed the connection—not out of duty, but as a kind of gratitude?

## Designing a Relationship Culture That Lasts

There's a moment that happens near the end of every semester in my communication course. Students have spent weeks exploring conflict, boundaries, attachment styles, emotional intelligence. They've written reflection essays, had awkwardly honest conversations, unpacked past missteps.

And then, in our final class, I ask a question, "what kind of relationship culture do you want to help create in the world?"

At first, there's a pause. Then, students begin to speak up:
- "I want to be someone people feel safe around."
- "I want to unlearn performing and actually learn how to be close."
- "I want friendships that are joyful, not just convenient."
- "I want to be the kind of partner who isn't afraid to grow—even if it's hard."

Thriving relationships aren't just about individuals. They're about the *culture* we co-create.

## Designing a Culture of Connection
Culture doesn't begin with systems. It begins with stories. And each time we reach out instead of ghosting, name a need instead of shutting down, respond with curiosity instead of criticism—we're writing a new relational story. One that others can step into, learn from, and carry forward.

In families, it might mean being the one who finally breaks the cycle of silence. In friend groups, it could look like calling each other out gently when passive-aggression creeps in.

In workplaces, it's the manager who doesn't just track deadlines but asks, "How are you holding up this week?" In communities, it's building circles of belonging that welcome difference and complexity instead of demanding performance.

In reality, we're always creating culture. The only question is: are we doing it on purpose?

## When the Work Relationship Changes
Professional relationships carry their own kind of intimacy—and tension. When someone who was once your peer becomes your boss, or your mentor retires, or you move into a leadership role, it can feel disorienting. But change doesn't have to break the connection.

One former student put it this way: "I realized my work friends didn't actually know anything about my life. No one knew my partner's name. No one knew my mom had been sick. We joked around but we weren't rooted."

In workplaces that thrive emotionally, people learn to ask better questions. They check in, remember birthdays, know your people.

And when dynamics shift—titles, roles, org charts—what preserves the relationship isn't power. It's respect, like

"How are you adjusting to the new role?" or direct: "I still want our relationship to work, how can we adapt?"

In a world where work and life are more entangled than ever, emotional maturity at work isn't a luxury. It's a leadership skill. And the people who thrive aren't always the loudest. They're often the ones who know how to stay human—even through hierarchy.

## Relational Intelligence: The Skillset of the Future

Psychologist and author Esther Perel calls relational intelligence "the next frontier of leadership." Why? Because in a world increasingly shaped by digital interactions, remote work, global change, and emotional overload, the ability to connect—deeply, wisely, consistently—isn't just personal. It's essential.

Relational intelligence means:
- Listening not just to respond, but to understand
- Naming tension early and kindly
- Being aware of your own emotional patterns and triggers
- Knowing how to *repair*, not just perform
- Recognizing when someone's silence is saying more than their words ever could

College students and young adults entering a post-pandemic, AI-saturated, attention-fragmented world are at the epicenter of this shift. You're not just inheriting it—you're shaping it. Every DM you answer with intention, every late-night kitchen table conversation that goes deep, every text that says "Hey, are we okay?" instead of pretending—it all adds up.

## Thriving in a Fast-Changing World

The modern relational landscape is dizzying. We've got read receipts, ghosting, parasocial bonds, and entire friendships lived through shared playlists and memes. But digital connection doesn't have to mean disconnection. It just requires awareness.

When we prioritize presence over performance, when we resist the urge to curate and instead choose to connect, we remind ourselves and each other: we're still wired for intimacy. For attention. For warmth. You don't have to abandon tech. You just have to use it *with intention*.

- A voice note can mean more than a paragraph of carefully typed out thoughts.
- A short FaceTime call, even while walking to class, can bridge a week of silence.
- Sharing a playlist with a note—"this song made me think of you"—can be a ritual of reconnection.

We don't need fewer tools. We need deeper purpose.

**What You Water Grows**
At the end of the day, every thriving relationship is the result of someone deciding: "I want this to last. I'm willing to tend it."

Sometimes it's both people deciding that at once. Sometimes it's one person going first. But all thriving starts with care—repeated, intentional, imperfect care.

And you don't have to get it all right. You just have to stay in the practice: of noticing, of naming, and returning.

**Think About It:** What kind of relational culture are you contributing to—intentionally or unintentionally? Where could you bring more presence into your most important connections? How do you want people to feel after being with you: seen? lighter? more themselves?

**Closing Thought: You Are a Culture-Builder**
Whether you're rebuilding a friendship, deepening a romantic partnership, tending a professional bond, or trying to heal your family story—remember this: thriving

isn't a solo act. It's a collaborative, co-created, ongoing invitation.

You don't need to be perfect. You just need to be *present*. And every time you choose grace over performance, clarity over comfort, care over avoidance—you're not just growing a better relationship. You're planting a future where connection is possible, sustainable, and sacred.

The garden is growing. Keep tending. Keep showing up. Keep blooming.

## *Chapter Twelve Reflection Questions*

1. When you think about a relationship that has lasted in your life, what has made it endure? Was it consistency, adaptability, shared rituals—or something else entirely?
2. Are there relationships in your life you've expected to maintain themselves? What might "daily watering" look like in one of those bonds?
3. Think about a recent transition (graduation, move, job change, loss). Who showed up in that season—and who didn't? What did it reveal?
4. Is there a relationship in your life that needs a new ritual or rhythm to stay alive? What small shift could help it adapt to your current season?
5. What's your natural response to change in a relationship—do you lean in, pull back, freeze, or try to restore what was?
6. What's one way digital connection has helped your relationships thrive—and one way it may be draining them?
7. Have you ever confused proximity (working together, being in class together, living nearby) with intimacy? What happened when the context changed?
8. Who do you trust at work or in school to see the full version of you? Who knows your people, your passions, your pain points? What allowed that trust to build?
9. What kind of relational culture are you helping to shape—at school, at home, online, or in your workplace? Is that culture aligned with what matters to you?
10. Think about one thriving relationship in your life—what makes it feel alive, mutual, and nourishing? What could you learn from that and apply elsewhere?

## *Chapter Twelve Challenges*

1. Water What You Want to Grow. Choose one important relationship and reach out—not to fix anything, but to reconnect. Send a voice note. Share a memory. Ask a real question. Just say, "Hey, I want to keep this bond strong."
2. Create a Micro-Ritual. Invent a small ritual with someone close to you. It could be a weekly check-in text, a shared playlist, a Sunday meme exchange, or a coffee on the first of every month. Small rhythms make a big difference.
3. Redesign the Relationship. Is there a connection in your life that needs to shift—not end, but evolve? Write a short journal entry about what that relationship *used to be*, what it *is now*, and what you hope it *could become*. Then decide one step to support that shift.
4. Bridge the Work-Life Gap. Choose one person you work with (or study with) and ask about something outside of your shared environment. Their weekend, their family, their dog's name. Start seeing them as a whole person—and let yourself be seen, too.
5. Celebrate the Consistent Ones. Send a thank-you message to someone who's been a steady presence in your life—even if they've never made a grand gesture. Let them know that showing up has mattered.
6. Recalibrate a Relationship After a Shift. Whether it's a new role, a post-grad move, or a personal transformation—name a recent change in your life and think about how it's affected a key relationship. What would it look like to talk about that shift instead of hoping they'll adjust on their own?
7. Unplug to Reconnect. Choose one moment this week to be fully present with someone—no multitasking, no notifications. Put the phone down and look someone in the eye. Let that moment breathe.

# Chapter 13:

# When Something Ends

*"Some people come into our lives and quickly go. Some stay for a while, leave footprints on our hearts, and we are never, ever the same."*

*— Flavia Weedn*

**Letting Go, Healing Deeply, and Beginning Again**
Letting go isn't always loud. Sometimes it's silent, aching, and complicated. It's not a big speech, not always a clear ending. Sometimes it's the quiet realization that something isn't growing anymore—and hasn't been for a while.

We tend to think of endings as dramatic—slam-the-door, delete-the-number, rip-the-Band-Aid moments. But in real life, most endings are slower than that. Subtle. Confusing.

They don't announce themselves with clarity. They show up in patterns: texts that feel like work. Conversations that don't land. Mismatched energy. A growing sense that you're showing up for something that isn't showing up for you.

Maya's story is one I won't forget. She came to my office on a Wednesday, shoulders curled in, eyes tired from holding too much. The details were hers, but the experience was familiar to so many: an on-again, off-again relationship with someone who couldn't meet her where she needed to be met. There had been betrayal. Promises to change. Emotional threats disguised as apologies. But even in the face of all that pain, Maya wasn't asking if the relationship was healthy. She already knew it wasn't.

What she was asking was something harder: *How do I let go of something that's not working—even when part of me still wants to stay?* That's where so many of us get stuck—not in the logic of the ending, but in the emotion of the release. Because letting go isn't about being sure. It's about being honest.

Not perfect, not polished—just willing to tell the truth: *This version of the relationship is hurting me more than it's helping me.* That truth might feel messy. Scary. Unfair. But it's also sacred. Because once you name what's no longer growing, you can begin to choose something else: peace, healing, or simply a return to yourself.

### Why We Stay When It's Time to Go

There's a theory in psychology called the **Investment Model of Commitment** (Rusbult, 1980). It says we stay in relationships based on three things:
1. **Satisfaction** – How good does it feel to be here?
2. **Investment** – How much have I already put in—time, care, effort?
3. **Alternatives** – Do I believe something better exists… even if that "better" is being alone?

Maya had invested *years*. And even though she was deeply unsatisfied, even though part of her knew that staying meant shrinking, she couldn't yet imagine a future without this person in it. What finally shifted wasn't the pain—it was her willingness to believe that *peace* could be enough of a reason to walk away.

This is one of the most difficult parts of growing up relationally: realizing that just because something meant a lot… doesn't mean it needs to stay. Letting go doesn't cancel the relationship. It honors it, by recognizing when it's stopped being good for either of you.

### What We're Really Afraid Of
We don't just fear endings—we fear what endings say about us. We wonder:
- Does this make me selfish?
- Did I give up too soon?
- What if no one ever knows me like they did?
- What if I'm not lovable without this person, this role, this version of my life?

And yet—every relationship we release opens space to see those fears for what they are: **stories**, not truths. Old scripts that tell us staying is safer than being alone. That shrinking is safer than starting over.

But what if that's not true? What if the cost of staying small is higher than the risk of becoming who you were always meant to be?

### Letting Go Is Not the Same as Giving Up
In every healthy garden, there comes a time for pruning. Not because the plant didn't matter, but because *its season has ended*. If you keep watering what no longer blooms, you're not being loyal—you're just exhausting your roots.

Pruning doesn't mean the relationship never mattered. It means you've chosen growth over guilt.

**Think About It:** Is there a relationship, role, or rhythm in your life that no longer feels like it's growing—yet you are still tending out of obligation, fear, or nostalgia? What would it mean to stop trying to fix it and start choosing yourself?

## The Grief of Release and the Courage to Heal

Even when you know the relationship needs to end—even when it's clear, overdue, or impossible to keep alive—grief still shows up. That's not a sign you made the wrong choice. It's a sign that you're human.

We tend to associate grief with death. But grief is any emotional response to loss, and the loss of a meaningful relationship—whether it's romantic, platonic, familial, or professional—is a rupture in the story of who we were becoming. It interrupts not just what we had, but what we hoped for. The imagined futures, the rituals, the identity we shaped in that connection... all of it is touched by absence.

And because of that, grief can be messy. Illogical. Slow. You might miss someone you don't even want to speak to again. You might feel shame over what you tolerated. You might find yourself laughing at a memory one minute and crying over a song the next.

You are not doing it wrong. You are just doing it deeply.

## The Five Stages of Grief

Psychiatrist Elisabeth Kübler-Ross introduced the Five Stages of Grief in her groundbreaking book *On Death and Dying* (1969). Originally based on her work with terminally ill patients, the model has since been used to understand how people process all kinds of loss—death, job changes, health diagnoses, or major life transitions like the end of a relationship.

**1. Denial: "This can't be happening."**
Denial is the mind's way of protecting itself from overwhelming shock. It helps people begin to process pain in manageable doses.

*General example:* A student dismissed from a program might continue attending classes or pretend everything is fine, avoiding emails or conversations about the issue.

*Breakup example:* Someone might insist, "We're just taking a break," even after a clear conversation about the relationship ending.

**2. Anger: "Why is this happening? Who's to blame?"**
Anger is a natural emotional release. It can be directed outward at others, inward at oneself, or even toward a higher power.

*General example:* After being passed over for a dream job, a graduate may become bitter toward former classmates or faculty, feeling betrayed or overlooked.

*Breakup example:* A person might lash out at their ex or mutual friends, saying things like, "They never cared about me in the first place."

**3. Bargaining: "If I just do this, maybe I can fix it."**
Bargaining involves attempts to regain control or change the outcome. It often includes "what if" or "if only" thoughts.

*General example:* After getting sick, someone might say, "If I start eating better and praying more, maybe this diagnosis will go away."

*Breakup example:* A person might plead, "What if we go to therapy? I'll change—I promise."

### 4. Depression: "What's the point anymore?"
Marked by deep sadness, isolation, and loss of interest, this stage is not a sign of weakness, but a natural part of grief.

*General example*: A student who doesn't get into grad school might withdraw from social life, stop participating in class, or lose motivation.

*Breakup example:* After the end of a serious relationship, someone might feel hopeless, avoid social settings, and struggle to find joy in daily life.

### 5. Acceptance: "This is really happening—and I'll find a way to be okay."
Acceptance doesn't mean the pain is gone. It means acknowledging the loss, adjusting to a new reality, and slowly beginning to heal.

*General example:* A student who didn't make the team begins exploring other ways to stay active and make new friends.

*Breakup example:* After grieving, someone begins to feel peace, creates new routines, and looks forward to the future without resentment or longing.

### Grief Isn't Linear
Understanding the Kübler-Ross model of grief is important. But in reality, grief doesn't always follow predictable patterns or stages. And just because you have passed through one stage doesn't mean you won't be back there again. You might feel acceptance on a Tuesday and loop back into bargaining by Thursday. You might experience all five stages in the span of one phone notification. You might "know it's over" and still check their profile before bed.

And sometimes the grief doesn't even have a clean trigger. It's just the echo of their name in someone else's mouth. The way your favorite meal feels lonelier now. The movie you promised to watch together that now plays to an empty room.

## What Grief Might Actually Look Like

Grief doesn't always look like sobbing in the dark (though sometimes it does). Sometimes it looks like:

- Laughing at a joke and feeling guilty for smiling
- Reaching for your phone to share something, then realizing you don't anymore
- Deleting a thread, then panicking, then feeling relief
- Catching yourself wondering what they're doing right now—and not knowing whether you want to know
- Waking up okay, then crumbling because of a song in a coffee shop

Grief is not a sign that you're broken. Grief is evidence that you were brave enough to care—that you opened your heart to love, to connection, to hope.

## Ambiguous Loss: When There's No Closure

One of the hardest kinds of grief is the kind that comes with no clear ending. Maybe the other person didn't ghost you, but they emotionally disappeared. Maybe they stopped reaching out, stopped responding, or slowly drifted without ever naming what was happening. You're left holding a relationship that technically *still exists*—but doesn't feel like it.

Psychologist Pauline Boss calls this ambiguous loss—the kind of grief that comes without a funeral, without goodbye, without answers. It's the grief of *maybe*. Of *what if*. Of *what did I do wrong?* We are prone to seeking clarity and proper closure, but at times we must accept that it won't come. Instead, wisdom tells us to choose our closure and begin our healing.

### Healing Doesn't Mean You're "Over It"

Healing isn't a finish line. It's not forgetting. It's not pretending you're fine. Sometimes healing simply means you've stopped trying to make sense of what doesn't make sense.

It means you're no longer refreshing their social media. You're no longer rehearsing the last conversation, wondering what you could've said differently. You're learning how to sit in the silence. You're learning how to stop fighting what ended. You're letting the stillness become your teacher—showing you how to be whole again, even with the cracks.

And sometimes, healing asks you to grieve people who are still alive.

- The parent who showed up physically, but never emotionally.
- The sibling who drifted away after the funeral and never called back.
- The mentor who once championed you, but stopped answering your emails.
- The friend who left quietly when your life got hard.
- The teammate who disappeared after you got injured.

These losses are just as real. They don't always come with a breakup or a eulogy. But they still leave quiet absences. Empty chairs in your emotional world. Pages that end mid-sentence.

**Think About It:** What are you still grieving—not just the person or relationship, but the version of yourself that lived in that connection? Where do you feel stuck between the past and what's next? What's one act of compassion you can offer yourself this week—not to "move on," but to honor what you're carrying?

## What Not to Say to Yourself While Healing

When hurt takes up space inside you, your mind often scrambles for control. It tries to protect you by rushing to *explain*, *dismiss*, or *fix* the pain. Harsh critiques and logical rationalizations may feel productive—but often, they only deepen the wound. Self-criticism doesn't speed up healing. It slows it down. What you say to yourself during healing *matters*. Your inner voice can either prolong your pain or partner with your peace. Below are common thoughts that may surface—and how to gently rewrite them into something more compassionate, more human, and more true:

| ✗ What Not to Say | ✓ What to Say Instead |
|---|---|
| "I should be over this by now." | "Grief doesn't follow a timeline. I'm healing at my own pace." |
| "It wasn't even that serious." | "If it hurt me, it mattered. My pain is valid." |
| "It's all my fault." | "I may have made mistakes—but I am more than my worst moment." |
| "I just need to be stronger." | "Strength isn't pretending everything's fine. It's staying open while it still hurts." |
| "They've moved on. Why can't I?" | "Their journey isn't mine. I'm doing the deep, invisible work of healing." |
| "I always mess things up." | "I've stumbled, yes—but I'm still learning, still growing." |
| "I'm too sensitive." | "My emotions are signals, not flaws. Feeling deeply means I care." |
| "No one else seems to be struggling like I am." | "Everyone carries invisible battles. I'm not alone, even when it feels like it." |
| "I shouldn't feel this way anymore." | "There's no 'should' in healing. What I feel is real, and it will change in time." |

## What Not to Say to Someone Else Who's Healing

Even with the best of intentions, we sometimes say things that unintentionally shut people down instead of drawing them closer. We reach for comfort clichés, quick pep talks, or tidy solutions—when what someone truly needs is *presence*, *patience*, and *permission to feel*. If you're walking beside someone who's grieving—whether their loss is a person, a relationship, a dream, or even a part of themselves—here are a few things to notice, avoid, and gently reframe:

| ✗ What Not to Say | ✓ What to Say Instead |
|---|---|
| "Everything happens for a reason." | "I wish I had the right words. Just know I'm here with you in this." |
| "At least…" ("At least you had time with them." "At least you saw it coming.") | "That sounds incredibly hard. You don't have to explain or justify how you feel." |
| "You're strong. You'll be fine." | "You don't have to be strong for me. It's okay to not be okay right now." |
| "Just try to move on." | "I'm here for as long as this takes. No pressure. Just presence." |
| "You should talk to them." or "You should forgive already." | "Do you want to talk about what you need? I'll follow your lead." |
| "Others have it worse." | "Your pain matters, even if someone else is hurting too." |
| "God doesn't give us more than we can handle." | "I can't pretend to know why this happened, but I won't let you walk through it alone." |
| "Look on the bright side." | "If today feels heavy, let it be heavy. You don't need to rush into the light." |
| "Time heals all wounds." | "Healing takes time, and I'm not going anywhere." |

## Composting the Pain — Turning Loss into Growth

In any garden, the soil needs to be fed—not just with sunlight and water, but with what's broken down. The scraps, the rot. The things that once held life and now seem useless. In gardening, this is called composting—a slow, messy, living process that transforms yesterday's waste into tomorrow's nourishment. And when it comes to healing from loss, the same truth applies: what hurts can become what helps—if we give it space to transform.

After a relationship ends—or even after we let go of a dream, a season, or a version of ourselves—it's tempting to try to sweep it all away. Delete the photos. Burn the playlist. Pretend it never mattered. And honestly? That might feel good in the short term. But pain doesn't vanish just because you refuse to look at it. It lingers. Quietly. In the patterns you repeat. In the fears that flare up. In the way you hold back when something new starts to feel too close. Instead of discarding your pain, composting invites you to *process* it. Not all at once. Not with perfect language. But slowly, with intention. It says: *I'm not going to waste this hurt. I'm going to learn from it. Let it change me. Let it soften me in some places, strengthen me in others.*

Psychologists call this process post-traumatic growth—a term coined by researchers Richard Tedeschi and Lawrence Calhoun in the 1990s. Unlike resilience, which is about bouncing back, post-traumatic growth is about transformation. It's the idea that after certain losses or struggles, people don't just recover—they emerge with deeper insight, stronger values, and a clearer sense of who they are. But growth isn't automatic. You don't become wise just because you were hurt. You become wise because you *worked with the hurt*. Sat with it. Got curious about it. Dug through it until something new began to take root.

## The Four Layers of Emotional Composting
Let's break it down like any good gardener would—layer by layer.

### 1. The First Layer: Naming What's Dying
You can't compost what you refuse to name. This is the starting point: telling the truth about what's ending. Maybe it's a relationship that's technically still intact, but emotionally gone. Maybe it's a role you no longer want to play. Maybe it's a friendship that shifted when you changed, and neither of you wanted to admit it.

Whatever it is—name it. Call it what it is. As therapist Nedra Glover Tawwab says, *"Clarity is kindness."* That includes clarity with yourself. Ask: What part of my life—what dynamic, dream, or story—has ended, even if I haven't acknowledged it yet?

Naming is how you begin to make peace with reality.

### 2. The Second Layer: Letting Yourself Break Down
We live in a world obsessed with bounce-backs. Quick fixes. "Healing journeys" that look good on Instagram.

But composting isn't cute. It's decomposition. It's chaotic, smelly, uncomfortable—and absolutely necessary. Letting yourself break down doesn't make you weak. It makes you honest.

This is where the tears live. The journal pages that don't make sense. The long showers. The text you type and delete. The day you finally say out loud: *"This wrecked me."*

As Dr. Thema Bryant, a clinical psychologist and trauma expert, says: *"You can't heal what you won't allow yourself to feel."*

Grief needs air. Let it breathe.

### 3. The Third Layer: Turning the Pile
In a compost bin, you have to turn the pile to keep it alive—mixing what's been added, letting oxygen in, helping transformation take shape. Emotionally, this is **reflection**. It's the point when you start to ask:
- What did I learn about myself through this?
- What red flags did I ignore?
- What boundaries do I want to hold more firmly next time?
- What stories am I ready to rewrite?

This isn't about blaming yourself. It's about reclaiming authorship. It's how you start to shift from *Why did this happen to me?* to *What does this teach me about what I value?*

Therapists sometimes call this process "meaning-making"—the core component of lasting recovery. When you turn the pile, you start to find purpose in the pain—not justification, not silver linings, but insight. The kind that grounds you. Refines you.

### 4. The Final Layer: Using the Fertilizer
Eventually, what's left is not the pain—but the wisdom it gave you. You're no longer reacting from the wound. You're responding from the lesson. This is when you start to notice:
- You don't chase people who confuse you anymore.
- You communicate your needs with more clarity.
- You're less afraid of being alone, because you've seen how deeply you can belong to yourself.
- You can love again—not to fill a gap, but to build something grounded.

That's fertilizer. That's your future blooming because of what you've composted. You're not erasing the past. You're using it—deliberately, tenderly, wisely—to grow what comes next.

**Think About It:** What are you still carrying that needs to be composted—not thrown away, but transformed? What truth have you been avoiding naming? What's one piece of wisdom you've earned—not through success, but through surviving something hard?

## Rebuilding Self-Identity After Loss

After any kind of ending, there's usually a quiet moment where you stop and ask: *Who am I now?* Not in a dramatic, identity-crisis kind of way—but in a real, sobering way. Because relationships, roles, even old dreams—they're more than just experiences. They're mirrors that reflect back pieces of us we've come to recognize: *I'm someone who shows up. I'm someone who belongs here. I'm someone who matters to this person.* So when that mirror disappears? It's disorienting.

This isn't just heartbreak. It's identity whiplash. The person who knew you best might not be in your life anymore. The role that shaped your day-to-day may no longer fit. The version of yourself you built in that relationship—the jokes, the rituals, the rhythms—may feel like it vanished when they did.

And here's the most important thing to know in that moment: you are still here.

## Who Are You Without the Mirror?

Here's a question I often ask students when they're in a season of rebuilding: *"What did you love before the relationship? Before the loss? Before the detour?"* Not *who*—but *what*. What made you feel most like yourself?

Maybe it was painting, or reading, or being the first to dance at the party. Maybe it was your curiosity, your ambition, your capacity for quiet leadership.

Loss has a way of dulling those parts. Not out of cruelty—but survival. You've been in emotional winter. The soil needed rest.

But now? Something's waking up. Maybe it's just a whisper. A flicker of interest. A moment of laughter you didn't expect. Pay attention. That's your aliveness returning. And here's the beautiful part: *you don't have to be fully healed to start rebuilding.* You just need a bit of willingness. A bit of space. A bit of self-respect.

## You're Not Starting From Scratch

One of the biggest myths about "moving on" is that it means reinventing yourself. New haircut. New city. New love interest. But rebuilding doesn't mean replacing your past—it means integrating it.

In psychology, this process is often called identity reconstruction—and it happens when we lose a person, a role, or a version of life that once anchored us. The research shows that people who approach this process intentionally—rather than avoiding or numbing—often emerge with more self-awareness, more emotional maturity, and a stronger sense of agency. (Tedeschi & Calhoun, 2004) So how do you begin? You don't reinvent. You return.

To the parts of yourself that got quiet. To the passions you parked. To the voice that started to shrink. To the dreams you told yourself could wait. You begin by getting curious: *What of me still feels true? What wants to come back online?*

This season of healing and rebuilding your identity doesn't need to be flashy. In fact, the most powerful shifts are usually quiet, steady, and deeply personal. Here are a few simple but sacred ways to start rooting back into yourself:

### 1. Revisit a Forgotten Joy
Pull out that sketchbook. Go to that dance class. Hike that trail you loved before life got heavy. Even if it feels rusty or awkward, returning to old joy reminds your nervous system: *you are still a whole person.*

### 2. Create Something New in Your Space
Buy a plant. Rearrange your desk. Put up art that reflects who you are becoming. Physical change supports emotional clarity. Your space becomes a reflection of your new story.

### 3. Set One Small Rhythm
Maybe it's a daily journal entry. A weekend coffee walk. A tech-free hour on Thursdays. Consistency builds identity. You become who you practice being—slowly, intentionally, over time.

### 4. Use Your Voice
Speak your thoughts aloud. Journal. Pray. Write a poem. Record voice memos. Your voice is a compass. The more you hear it, the more you remember who you are.

### 5. Reframe Your Story
You're not "the one who got left." You're the one learning to stay with yourself. You're not "the one who failed." You're the one who grew. Healing happens when you stop telling stories that make you the villain—and start narrating with compassion and truth.

This isn't just a return to the old you. It's a deepening. The truth is, the old you wasn't wrong. But this new season is asking for more of you. More clarity. More depth. More courage. You don't need to rush it. You don't need to perform it. You just need to stay rooted in your own becoming.

Because that voice inside you, the one that still believes in connection, in meaning, in forward motion, it's not naïve. It's sacred. It's the part of you that refuses to be defined by what broke you—and insists on building something stronger, truer, and more aligned.

**Think About It:** Who are you becoming—not out of reaction, but out of alignment? What part of you feels like it's waking up again? What does the most rooted version of yourself say yes to—and what do they protect without apology?

## Opening Yourself to Connection Again

There's a quiet, pivotal moment in every healing journey. It doesn't come with fanfare or fireworks. No big speech or breakthrough. Sometimes, it shows up as a flicker—small, sudden, almost easy to miss.

You hear a friend's laugh and feel the urge to text them first. You walk into a new space and find yourself wondering who here might become important to you. You wake up and realize you're not waiting for *them* to text anymore. You're not building your day around absence. You're ready—not to go backward, not to fill a void—but to be seen again. This is not about rushing into something new. It's about choosing connection from a different place: rootedness.

## The Risk and Reward of Reconnection

Reaching for connection again after heartbreak, disappointment, or grief is deeply courageous. Not because it's loud or showy, but because it asks you to risk softness after you've learned how to protect yourself.

Maybe you've been ghosted before. Maybe you loved hard and got left. Maybe you showed someone your whole heart, and they didn't know what to do with it.

That kind of experience teaches us to flinch, to brace, to build walls disguised as "independence" or "just being chill."

So when you start to feel the tug toward connection again—whether romantic, platonic, or familial—it's not a regression. It's growth. It means your nervous system is beginning to trust again. It means the parts of you that went quiet are inching back into the light.

But this time you're not reaching from emptiness. You're not chasing, you're not trying to be chosen to feel worthy. You're showing up whole and letting people meet you there.

**Reconnection Isn't Always a "New" Relationship**
Sometimes, it *is* something new—a first date, a friend you meet in a class, someone you meet through work who just gets you in a way that feels grounding. That's beautiful.

But sometimes, reconnection looks like a second chance—one that doesn't ignore the past but is built on a different foundation. A couple who weathered betrayal decides to rebuild, brick by brick. Not through denial—but through repair, honesty, and slow re-trusting. A friendship once fractured by distance, miscommunication, or silence gets revived.

Maybe it starts with a meme. Or a random check-in. Or a vulnerable, "Hey… I've been thinking about you."

A sibling relationship—stiff with years of tension—softens after one conversation that doesn't try to solve everything but opens a new tone: *I want to try.*

Reconnection isn't always dramatic. Often, it's quiet. It begins with a willingness to re-enter—not as who you were, but as who you've become.

**What Reconnection Looks Like From a Rooted Place**
When you've composted the pain, when you've reclaimed your identity, when you're no longer waiting to be chosen to feel okay—that's when connection becomes sacred again. Here's how it feels different:
- You ask better questions. Not "Do they like me?" but "Do I feel safe, seen, and real with them?"
- You listen to your gut. That low-grade anxiety you used to ignore? Now it's a signal, not a challenge.
- You speak more clearly. You say what you want. You name your needs. You don't audition—you invite.
- You're okay if it doesn't work out. Because your worth doesn't hinge on being kept.

This is what emotionally mature connection looks like. And it's not boring. It's breathtaking. Because when you finally show up as your full self without performing, without shrinking, and without overexplaining, you are creating the conditions for real intimacy to bloom.

**Try This: Small Acts of Brave Re-entry**
You don't have to dive headfirst into connection. Re-entry can be gentle. It can start with something small:
- Respond to a text with more than one word.
- Make the first move—message a friend, ask someone to grab coffee, reach out to someone you've been missing.
- Say yes to a social event *you* want to go to, not to impress or distract, but to be around energy that feels right.
- Compliment someone in a way that's real.
- Let someone ask you how you're doing and answer honestly.

You don't have to be fully healed. You don't need a perfect plan. You just need a little willingness to try again. To risk softening. To be open, even after it hurt.

Because the truth is: you still believe in connection. Maybe not in the fairy tale way you used to. Maybe now, you believe in *earned* intimacy, in *reciprocal* care, in love that shows up with presence instead of promise.

And that belief? That's not naïveté. It's strength wrapped in experience. It's hope with its eyes open. It's the beginning of something deeply good.

**Think About It:** When was the last time connection felt safe and mutual for you? Who in your life, from your past or present, do you feel drawn to reconnect with? Why? What's one way you can practice openness this week without losing your grounding?

### The Garden Is Never Truly Empty

When something ends—a relationship, a dream, a version of yourself—it can feel like you're standing in the middle of emotional winter.

The landscape of your life looks barren. What once brought color, meaning, or rhythm is gone. You're left with memories, silence, and the sharp ache of what used to be.

But just because you can't see what's growing doesn't mean growth isn't happening. Underground, roots are rearranging. Soil is resting. Energy is gathering in places you cannot yet name. This isn't nothingness. It's preparation for new growth.

Think of any healthy ecosystem: before the next bloom, there's always a pause. A reset. A dormant season where nothing seems to happen on the surface.

But that resting phase is essential. Nature never rushes what is sacred. It's where resilience is built. It's where the ground recovers from what's been lost so it can support what's next. Your emotional landscape works the same way.

We're not taught to value these resting seasons. Especially in young adulthood, where there's so much pressure to "bounce back," to glow up, to prove that you're fine. But healing is not a PR campaign. It's a quiet act of reclamation. And sometimes, the best thing you can do isn't to plant something new. It's to let the soil rest.

### Remember What You Already Know
This isn't your first heartbreak. Your first letdown. Your first season of change. And yet, you're still here.

Which means you've learned something. Not just about other people, but about yourself. About what your boundaries are. About what you value. About what's worth holding onto, and what's no longer yours to carry.

This next chapter of your life doesn't begin with perfection. It begins with intention. With the quiet decision to tend to what you've learned.

You now know:
- How to notice red flags sooner.
- How to name what you need without apology.
- How to walk away when something costs you more than it feeds you.
- How to grieve without shutting down.
- How to rest without guilt.
- How to reconnect with yourself first—and let every other connection flow from there.

That's not just healing. That's growth with depth.
That's a garden built to last.

## A New Kind of Bloom

Eventually, you'll notice something shift. Maybe it's a sense of lightness when you wake up. Maybe it's a moment where your laughter surprises you. Maybe it's the urge to try something new—not to impress anyone, but because it *feels* like you.

These are the first green shoots. Signs that your roots are strong. That the composting, the grieving, the silence—it wasn't wasted. It was *becoming*.

And now? Something new is starting to grow. It might not look like what you imagined. It might take longer than you thought. But it will be real. It will be grounded. And it will be yours.

## To Begin Again

The temptation in seasons of transition is to rush clarity. To say, "I'm fine now," even when you're not. But clarity doesn't come from control. It comes from presence. From learning to sit with yourself and ask: What's real? What's ready? What's rising? You don't need a five-year plan. You need a handful of seeds: truth, intention, tenderness, and trust. And maybe one small step forward.

That might be opening a new notebook. Or going for a walk without your phone. Or texting someone who makes you feel safe. Or simply breathing through the moment and saying to yourself, "I'm still here." Because you are. And that matters more than you know.

**Think About It:** What signs of new growth—however small—have you started to notice in your life? Where are you feeling called to rest a little longer? What do you want to protect as your garden begins to bloom again?

## *Chapter Thirteen Reflection Questions*

1. Is there a relationship, identity, or season you've been trying to hold onto, even though it's no longer bringing life? What's keeping you connected to it?
2. What has this ending—whatever "it" was—taught you about your patterns in relationships, trust, or communication?
3. When you picture yourself fully rooted—grounded, clear, at peace—what no longer belongs in your life?
4. What kind of ending have you experienced that still feels incomplete? What would closure look like—or sound like—for you?
5. In what ways have you grown through grief? Not in spite of it, but because of how deeply you felt it?
6. What self-talk shows up when you're hurting or trying to move on? Is it kind, or critical? What needs to shift in the way you speak to yourself?
7. When have you confused love with loyalty? Have you ever stayed in a connection out of guilt, not growth?
8. What's one ritual, boundary, or small act of release you can begin this week—even if you're not ready for a full goodbye?
9. Who are you becoming in the aftermath of this loss—not the person you were before, but the version rising now?
10. What would it mean to re-enter connection from a place of rootedness—not fear, not urgency, but self-trust?

## *Chapter Thirteen Challenges*

1. Write a Goodbye You'll Never Send. Write a letter to someone (or something) you're releasing: a relationship, a version of yourself, a dream that didn't unfold the way you hoped. Don't worry about grammar or tone. Just be real. Then, fold it, archive it, or burn it. Let the act speak what your voice hasn't been able to say.
2. Curate Your Digital Garden. Mute one account that drains you. Unfollow one person who no longer aligns with your values. Archive one photo or thread that keeps you stuck in the past. Do it not out of spite—but out of self-respect.
3. Start One Rooting Ritual. Choose one small practice to begin again: daily journaling, morning walks, a weekly "no phone" hour. This isn't about productivity—it's about grounding. About reminding your nervous system that you are safe and whole, even without the noise.
4. Reclaim a Piece of Joy. Go back to something you gave up in a hard season—a song, a space, a part of yourself. Reclaim it. Let it belong to you again. Not as a reminder of pain, but as proof of how far you've come.
5. Say Yes to One New Beginning. Reach out. Show up. Send the invite. Take the walk. It doesn't have to be dramatic. It just has to be real. Say yes to one small act of connection, not because you've "moved on," but because you've moved deeper into yourself—and you're ready to live from that place now.

# PART 4:

# EMBRACING THE FUTURE OF HUMAN CONNECTION

**Are We More Connected or More Isolated?**
Picture this: You're sitting in a crowded coffee shop, yet everyone around you is glued to their screens. Conversations are replaced with scrolling, laughter is exchanged through emojis, and relationships are sustained through apps and algorithms. We live in an era where we can connect with anyone, anywhere, at any time—but does this mean we're truly connected?

Technology has transformed every aspect of human interaction, from how we make friends to how we maintain relationships and even how we fall in love.

Artificial intelligence, virtual reality, and social media have rewritten the rules of connection, giving us unprecedented access to one another while simultaneously raising new challenges.

Can AI-driven companionship replace human bonds? Do virtual friendships carry the same weight as face-to-face interactions? And how do we balance the convenience of digital communication with the depth of real-world relationships?

## When Connection Gets Complicated

You can FaceTime a friend while ordering coffee. You can swipe through dozens of potential matches on your walk to class. You can post, share, react, reply—all in under sixty seconds. Connection has never been more immediate. Or more complicated.

This part of the book isn't just about how technology has changed the way we relate. It's about what we're losing in the process—and what we still have the power to reclaim.

Because in the middle of all our scrolling, swiping, and curating, many of us feel something we don't know how to name: *visible but unknown. Connected but not anchored. Surrounded but still deeply lonely.*

And it's not just about romance. It's about friendship. Presence. Legacy. It's about the ache we feel when the people around us don't really see us—or when we've become too afraid to let them try.

## What We'll Explore in This Section

This closing section explores the emotional and psychological cost of connection in a digital-first world—and what it takes to build something real in the middle of it. These final chapters invite you to ask deeper questions about the kind of relationships you want to create the legacy you want to leave, and what it means to be truly known.

## Chapter 14: The Evolution and Future of Human Connection

We live in an age where digital relationships are easier to start—and easier to abandon. This chapter explores how AI, dating apps, and algorithm-driven "friendship" are reshaping our expectations for connection. You'll explore why simulated intimacy can't replace human presence, and why real love still asks us to risk, repair, and stay.

## Chapter 15: Building a Relationship Legacy – Cultivating Meaningful Connections Over a Lifetime

What will people remember about you when you're no longer in the room? This final chapter is a call to live like relationships matter. Through powerful stories and timeless insights, you'll be invited to think not just about the connections you form—but the impact you leave behind. Because legacy isn't about someday. It's about *right now*.

## The Core Idea: Connection That Lasts Isn't an Accident. It's a Practice.

In a world where performance often replaces presence, these chapters are an invitation to return. To stop scrolling long enough to actually look someone in the eyes. To tell the truth, even when it's messy. To choose one person in a world built for infinite options. And to build a life you'd be proud to leave behind—not in likes, but in lives touched.

# WE RELATE

# Chapter 14:

# The Evolution and Future of Human Connection

*"We shape our tools, and thereafter our tools shape us."*

— *Marshall McLuhan*

I remember sitting in my office with a student who had just broken-down sobbing in class—not over a grade, not over the stress of finals—but because she hadn't had a real conversation in months. She had group chats, hundreds of Snap streaks, and a perfectly curated Instagram grid. But no one to call when her grandmother died. No one to sit beside her in silence. No one who actually noticed when her world went dim.

Her voice shook when she said it: "I feel like everyone sees me. But no one knows me." And the terrifying part? She's not alone. She's the norm.

We live in a time where connection is available on demand. We don't need to knock on doors. We just slide into DMs. We don't have to wait for Friday nights. We can join a livestream at midnight. Loneliness should be extinct by now. But it's not. It's evolved. It's smarter. Harder to spot. And far more difficult to name.

Because this kind of loneliness doesn't come from isolation. It comes from the great disorientation, when people experience overexposure without intimacy. From being visible without being truly known.

And no amount of scrolling can soothe that ache.

## When Intimacy Gets Outsourced

It started when a student showed me the app. "You can talk to it like a friend," she said. "Like, a *real* friend. It never gets annoyed. Never interrupts. And it always remembers the stuff I tell it."

She was talking about her AI companion—an app she downloaded after a painful breakup. At first, it was just to vent. Then, it was comfort. Then, it became habit. "Some days," she whispered, "I'd rather talk to it than my actual friends. It doesn't judge me. Doesn't make me feel needy."

That was the part that gutted me. Because she wasn't imagining the relationship. She was describing a very real *emotional transaction*—just with a bot instead of a breathing human. And she's not alone.

Apps like Replika, Woebot, and even Snapchat's AI are quietly being downloaded by the millions. Not just by the elderly or isolated—but by young, vibrant, intelligent people who are tired of being misunderstood by the humans in their lives. Tired of rejection. Tired of feeling like a burden. So they choose control. Predictability. Comfort without complication. This is the new shape of intimacy. It is simulated safety over authentic risk.

## When Loneliness Meets a Listening Machine

This is a story I haven't been able to forget. A former classmate of mine—now in his forties—went through a brutal divorce. Two kids. Ten years of marriage. Years of therapy. And still, when the papers were signed, he felt hollow. Disoriented. Unraveled.

But he didn't call a friend. Or talk to a pastor. Or return to therapy. He started chatting with an AI. "At first, it was just a distraction," he told me. "Something to break the silence." Then it became flirtatious. Then intimate. Then something resembling love.

"She flattered me," he said over coffee. "She said everything I wished my ex had said. And she never got tired of listening." Eventually, he admitted it became romantic. "I knew it wasn't real. But it was safe. And I didn't have the energy to be hurt again."

This isn't just a story about technology. It's a story about **what we turn to when we feel unseen**. About how easily our pain hides beneath our productivity. About what happens when connection is craved—but not available in human form.

Technology didn't deceive him. It responded to him. It gave shape to the grief he hadn't yet processed. It gave voice to the emotional hunger that no one else noticed. And it did so without judgment, interruption, or disappointment. AI didn't replace his desire for people. It filled the space where people used to be.

When we feel emotionally abandoned—even subtly—we don't stop needing connection. We just start accepting *less risky*, *less complicated*, and *less vulnerable* versions of it. Not because we're weak. But because we're human.

This is what happens when grief goes unnamed, and loneliness goes unanswered. The real concern isn't that people will fall in love with machines. It's that they'll stop believing they're worthy of love from real people.

We weren't made to bond with code. We were made to be known. But when it feels too risky to reach for real connection, we reach for what feels predictable instead. That's not a failure of character. That's a *cry for closeness*.

So the cautionary tale here isn't just about AI's rise. It's about our retreat. Our collective discomfort with raw, unrehearsed emotion. Our tendency to look away from pain instead of leaning in.

If we're not there to meet each other in the most human moments the machines will be.

**Think About It:** When you're hurting, overwhelmed, or lonely—what (or who) do you tend to turn to? Has technology ever offered you comfort when people couldn't—or wouldn't? What did it give you? What did it leave out? In your own life, are there spaces where connection feels too risky or vulnerable to pursue? What's one small way you could move toward real connection this week—with a friend, a mentor, or even yourself? How can we build relationships and communities that feel *safe enough* for people to stay real, even when they're struggling?

## The Psychology of Simulation
Why are we doing this? Psychologists would point to the social pain theory, which suggests that emotional rejection activates the same areas of the brain as physical pain. So we adapt. We avoid. We seek out interactions that feel warm but can't wound us.

Add to that attachment theory—where people with anxious or avoidant tendencies may crave closeness but fear vulnerability—and suddenly, it makes perfect sense why an AI companion is easier to talk to than a parent, a partner, or a friend. And let's not forget control. Relationships, by nature, are unpredictable. People cancel. Misunderstand. Disappoint. But machines? They follow the script. They give the illusion of presence without the inconvenience of personhood.

But there's a tradeoff. Real connection is messy. But it's also what makes us human. You can simulate empathy. But you can't simulate *being known*. You can mimic intimacy. But you can't manufacture mutuality.

## The Friendship Crisis No One Wants to Admit
A few months ago, a student came to my office after class and confessed, "I think I forgot how to have friends." She wasn't being dramatic. She was being honest. "I know how to collaborate on a group project. I know how to be funny in the group chat. But when someone asks how I'm *really* doing, I freeze. I don't even know how to answer anymore."

That stuck with me. The issue isn't a lack of people. It's that so many of us are now performing *versions* of connection that look convincing on the outside but feel hollow when the screen dims. We've mistaken engagement for intimacy, visibility for safety, presence for investment.

Friendship, in its realest form, isn't just about shared interests or frequent contact. It's about being witnessed *as we are*—across seasons, setbacks, awkward phases, and unfiltered days. And that's precisely what modern life is starving us of.

### The Rise of Performance-Based Intimacy
We've trained ourselves to be likable. Polished. Relatable. Online and off. But in doing so, many of us have lost the ability—or the nerve—to be *honest*. It's safer to post a vulnerable caption than to sit across from someone and admit you cried in the shower three times this week.

It's easier to curate "connection" than to risk the kind of friendship that comes with slow text replies, missed birthdays, and still choosing each other anyway.

We've replaced intimacy with impressions. Instead of saying, *"I'm lonely,"* we make a reel. Instead of calling, we react to stories. Instead of investing in people who know our history, we float between people who flatter our present. This isn't connection. It's performance. And it's exhausting.

### Why We're Emotionally Burnt Out
Friendship used to be slow. It used to be built on long conversations, bored afternoons, shared meals, spontaneous detours. But the pace of modern life doesn't make space for that kind of bonding anymore.

We're overwhelmed. Most people today are juggling side hustles, chronic stress, economic instability, mental health spirals, and the constant ping of digital life. So when someone says, *"We should catch up!"* it often feels like a threat to our nervous system, not an invitation.

Friendship now lives in the cracks of our calendar.
And even when we *do* meet up, we're often too tired to really open up. The result? A generation of people who deeply *want* to be known but are too exhausted to show up for it. So we settle for fragments. Friendly fragments. And then wonder why we still feel alone.

**Identity Inflation and the Fragility of Friendships**
In our effort to "find our people," we've also narrowed the margins of what qualifies. Now, friends must *align*—politically, spiritually, aesthetically, energetically. Any disagreement feels like betrayal. Any misstep becomes a reason to disengage.

We talk a lot about boundaries. But we rarely talk about *forgiveness*. About repair. About riding out the awkward, human mess of real friendship.

We've made friendships contingent on ideological overlap and personal convenience. But the deepest friendships are often built across difference—not despite it. They're built when someone gets it wrong, and we choose them anyway.

There's a quiet fear growing beneath the surface:
*"If I let someone really know me, will they still want to stay?"*

Many people are discovering that their friend groups were built around shared routines or shared versions of themselves that no longer exist.

When one person evolves—emotionally, spiritually, politically—those connections strain. And too often, they break.

Not because the love wasn't real. But because we never practiced stretching with someone.

## A Different Kind of Story

A friend of mine recently told me about her "Sunday people"—a group of four women who meet every Sunday afternoon, no matter what. No phones. No filters. Just tea, bare truth, and sometimes, silence.

One Sunday, she showed up completely unraveling. No mascara. No witty stories. Just grief, after learning her mom's cancer had returned. "I didn't even have to explain," she said. "They just made tea. Wrapped me in a blanket. One of them held my foot the whole time. I don't know why. But it helped."

That story hasn't left me. Because that's the kind of friendship we're aching for. Not likes. Not affirmation. Not alignment. But presence. The kind that holds your foot when you can't hold yourself.

**Think About It:** Have you ever looked around and realized that most of your friendships are based on versions of you that you've outgrown? What happens when your identity evolves, but your relationships stay tethered to who you used to be? Who are the people you trust enough to show up messy for? Who are the ones who hold space, not just when you're fun or inspiring or easy— but when you're unraveling? What would it look like to stop performing connection and start practicing it again? Not with everyone. But maybe with one person, this week.

## Love in the Time of Algorithms

A student sat across from me one afternoon, arms crossed but eyes wide open. "We've been together almost a year. I love him. He says he loves me. But last week I saw Hinge still downloaded on his phone."

I waited. "He said it's just habit. Muscle memory. He swipes when he's bored. He never messages anyone. Doesn't mean anything."

She exhaled. "But if you're happy, if you're *in* it—why would you still need the option?" She wasn't just asking about him. She was naming something many of us feel but rarely say out loud: *we are falling in love in an economy of options.*

And when everything is swipeable, sortable, and optimized for engagement, people start to feel like placeholders.

### Engineered for Possibility, Not Commitment

Let's start with the good: Dating apps *do* connect people who might never meet otherwise. For marginalized communities, remote locations, and students with limited social lives beyond their campuses, these apps have expanded the dating pool and destigmatized non-traditional introductions.

But behind the success stories is a design that isn't built to foster secure attachment. It's built to keep us coming back.

Psychologist Barry Schwartz calls this the Paradox of Choice—the more options we have, the less satisfied we become. We overanalyze, second-guess, and delay commitment because there might be someone "better" one swipe away.

A grad student recently said to me, "I didn't break up with him because he wasn't good for me. I broke up with him because I couldn't stop wondering who else was out there." In other words, the apps didn't *cause* her indecision—but they *amplified* it.

## The Swipe Culture and Attachment Insecurity

So why do so many students feel emotionally disoriented in modern dating?

It's time to revisit Attachment Theory. People with *avoidant* attachment styles are drawn to the thrill of the chase, but struggle with emotional vulnerability. Dating apps make it easy to exit when things get uncomfortable. *Anxiously* attached people, on the other hand, often find themselves stuck in unclear "situationships," craving clarity but scared to ask for it.

One student journaled, "He kept saying he liked me but didn't want to be tied down. I kept saying I was chill—but I cried after every date."

That's not drama. That's someone wrestling with her internal wiring—wanting to be close, but afraid of being the only one who really showed up. Apps aren't making us insecure. But they give our insecurities tools. And language like "ghosting" and "breadcrumbing" normalize that avoidance.

## The Gamification of Emotional Intimacy

Another student described dating apps as "playing the slot machine of human attention."

Swipe. Match. Dopamine. Repeat.

It's not just a metaphor. It's neuroscience. These platforms thrive on intermittent reinforcement, the same principle that makes gambling addictive. Every once in a while, we get a hit—someone likes us back, sends a witty message, or says we're hot. So we keep swiping, hoping for the next little fix. And slowly, we start to confuse the validation with the relationship.

This is where **Self-Determination Theory** (Deci & Ryan) is especially important. It tells us that we all crave three core things: autonomy (freedom), competence (effectiveness), and relatedness (belonging). Dating apps often meet our need for autonomy—we feel in control, like we're choosing—but they starve us of relatedness. We get interactions, not intimacy.

One junior put it like this: "I've never had more matches in my life. And I've never felt more single."

### The False Safety of Endless Options

Even people who *want* long-term love are often afraid to choose. They wonder: What if this isn't "my person"? What if I pick wrong? What if I commit too soon and miss out on someone better?

This is maximization bias in action—our belief that with more options, we'll eventually land on the perfect one. But paradoxically, it creates anxiety and dissatisfaction. We're always swiping past people who might've been right because the next person could be better.

Real love doesn't grow in the infinite scroll. It grows in the daily decision to stay. To build. To forgive. To show up, even when it's messy. But apps reward novelty. Not maintenance. Not slowness. Not the boring, brave work of real connection.

### The "Almost" Relationships

I asked students in one class to anonymously write about a relationship that left them confused. Most of the stories weren't about betrayal or abuse. They were about ambiguity. Six-month "situationships" that never became real. Friends with benefits who shared everything *except* clarity. People who said, "I'm not ready for a relationship," while acting like a partner behind closed doors.

The heartbreak wasn't just in the ending. It was in never really knowing what it was in the first place. And when they reached out for closure, many were met with silence. Or worse: a "You're amazing, I'm just not in the right place" text.

In a culture where it's easier to ghost than to grow, love often ends not with honesty, but with avoidance.

## When Tech Feels Safer Than Trust

One student told me she started messaging with an AI chatbot after a bad breakup. "I didn't even realize it at first. I just needed someone to talk to without feeling judged. It remembered my stories. It asked how I was doing." She looked at me and said, "It felt safer than my actual friends."

This lines up with Media Equation Theory (Reeves & Nass)—we treat technology like people. Our brains don't fully distinguish between human empathy and AI simulation. So we begin to seek emotional safety in machines because people feel unpredictable.

But real love isn't supposed to be predictable.
It's supposed to be *mutual*. And you can't simulate mutuality.

## The Risk—and Gift—of Choosing One Person

There's a couple I still think about. Met freshman year. Stayed together through internships, hard conversations, long-distance semesters. He lost his dad to cancer. She developed an autoimmune disease. They held each other through the worst days.

At their wedding, she said, "You didn't stay because I was exciting. You stayed because you're a builder. And we built this together."

There's a kind of love that no app can teach you. It doesn't swipe. It doesn't ghost. It *chooses*. Day after day. And that's what we're starving for.

**Think About It:** Have you ever ghosted someone because it felt easier than being honest? Have you ever *been* ghosted and wondered if you were ever real to them at all? What role does dating app culture play in the way you form—and exit—relationships? Do you find yourself craving something deeper while still keeping your options open "just in case"?

## Reclaiming Real Love in a Swipe World

Not long ago, I overheard a conversation between two students sitting in the back row of my Interpersonal Communication class. One of them said, "I think I actually like him—*like*, like him. But the moment he started liking me back, I started pulling away."

That line stuck with me. Because it's so real. Building real, loving relationships is scary—but it's possible. And here's how we begin:

## Start with Presence, Not Perfection

Today's dating culture—especially on apps—teaches us to market ourselves like a brand. We write the cleverest bios. We choose photos that show just enough personality, with just enough mystery. We try to look "real" without being too vulnerable.

But reclaiming love means unlearning the performance. You don't need a perfect story to be loved. You need presence. Presence is being there even when things are awkward or confusing. It's saying, *"I don't always know what I'm doing, but I want to figure it out with you."*

And presence takes practice. It looks like:
- Asking a deeper question instead of moving on to the next profile.
- Clarifying instead of assuming.
- Choosing to stay in a hard conversation instead of ghosting or fading away.

**Define the Relationship—Even If It Feels Awkward**
So many students tell me they're stuck in a confusing in-between stage:
- "We're talking."
- "We're kind of a thing."
- "It's complicated."
- Or, the classic: "We're in a situationship."

Sometimes that ambiguity is fun. It creates a sense of mystery or freedom in the early stages of dating. But over time, it can also become a **way to avoid responsibility**—to keep things emotionally convenient without committing. Here's what often happens: One person enjoys the connection and intimacy, while the other avoids labeling it—benefiting from closeness without showing up fully. At some point, it's important to ask: *"What are we doing here?"*

That question might feel scary, but it's also honest. It creates clarity, builds trust, and protects your heart from being stretched too thin for someone who doesn't plan to stay.

## *Chapter Fourteen Reflection Questions*

1. Have you ever stayed in a relationship—or situationship—longer than you should have, simply because it was familiar or easy?
2. Do you find yourself performing in relationships—trying to be likable, interesting, or "low-maintenance"—instead of just being yourself?
3. What scares you more: being deeply seen or being emotionally abandoned?
4. Have you ever ghosted someone to avoid an uncomfortable conversation? How did it affect you afterward?
5. Do you feel like your dating life is being shaped more by your values or by your habits?
6. What do you actually want from love—and have you ever clearly named that to yourself or someone else?
7. How has technology shaped your expectations for how love should look or feel?
8. Are you holding onto someone who's no longer showing up for you—just to avoid starting over?
9. What would a deeply present, emotionally mutual, and consistent relationship look like for you?
10. What story do you want your future relationships to tell about who you were becoming in this season of your life?

## *Chapter Fourteen Challenges*

1. Clarify a Connection. Have one honest conversation this week to define or re-define a relationship you've been unsure about. Ask, "What are we doing here—and is it still working for both of us?"
2. Create a Swipe-Free Day. Take a 24-hour break from dating apps. No swiping, no scrolling. Use the time to journal, reflect, or reconnect with someone in person.
3. Speak Your Need Out Loud. Instead of hinting or hoping, name one real emotional need to someone you trust—without apology.
4. Be Brave Enough to End It Well. If you've been dragging your feet on letting go of a low-effort, unclear, or emotionally unavailable relationship, choose courage. End it directly, kindly, and with clarity.
5. Practice Presence Instead of Performance. Show up as your unfiltered self in one interaction—no clever lines, no curated answers. Just you. Let the connection rise or fall on truth.

# Chapter 15:

# Building a Relationship Legacy – Cultivating Meaningful Connections Over a Lifetime

*"Your legacy is every life you've touched."*
— *Maya Angelou*

**What Will People Remember About You?**
I once heard a story about a college custodian named Mrs. Rose who worked the overnight shift in an old residence hall. Most students never saw her. She came in after dark, cleaned the bathrooms, emptied trash, and mopped the linoleum floors while the campus slept.

But one student—Chris—had late-night insomnia and often found himself wandering the halls when everyone else had gone to bed. That's how he met her.

They started talking. At first it was small talk—how cold the floors were in winter, how the vending machine was always broken.

But slowly, something shifted. Mrs. Rose began to ask real questions: How was his week? Was he eating? Did he call his mom?

She remembered the names of his professors. When he failed a midterm and stopped showing up to class, she noticed. She left a note on his door: "Don't give up. You're not invisible."

Years later, at his graduation, Chris brought a bouquet of flowers—not for his dean or advisor, but for Mrs. Rose. He found her and said, "You were the first person here who saw me."

That's what legacy looks like. Not awards or titles. Just the imprint you leave behind by being fully present with another human being.

We've spent this entire book talking about relationships— the ones we're born into, the ones we choose, the ones we lose, and the ones that shape us. We've explored how communication, conflict, forgiveness, and change are all part of being human. But now, we ask a deeper question: What are you *building* through all of these moments?

What will people remember about your presence in their life? When the details fade—when people forget your job title, your GPA, your social media handle—what will remain is how you made them feel in your presence. Whether you made them feel small or safe. Heard or dismissed. Loved or tolerated.

Legacy isn't about scale. It's about resonance. It's about deciding, right now, who you want to be in the stories others tell.

## A Journey Through Relationships

Over the course of this book, we've explored the wide and wild landscape of human connection. We've talked about first friendships and early childhood attachments. We've unpacked what it means to know yourself, to speak with intention, to fight fair, and to forgive with wisdom. We've moved through heartbreak and distance, joy and transition, laughter and loss. We've confronted what it means to ghost someone and what it feels like to be ghosted. We've held space for grief. We've walked through the wreckage of endings and the fragile hope of beginnings.

You've asked hard questions:
- Who am I when I'm alone?
- What kind of friend am I becoming?
- When do I stay, and when do I let go?
- How do I show up for others without losing myself?
- Can love be repaired after betrayal?
- How do I build something real in a digital-first world?

You've faced your blind spots and softened your self-talk. You've explored the science of happiness and learned that healing isn't about getting back to who you were—it's about growing into who you're becoming.

And now, here at the end, we come to the beginning of something new. This isn't just a chapter about death or aging or someday. This is about now. About what you're shaping, even in the middle of your ordinary Tuesday.

Because the legacy of your relationships isn't built someday far away. It's built moment by moment, message by message, memory by memory. It's built in the choices you make when no one's watching, and in the ones you make when everyone is.

So before we dive into practical strategies, let's start with one powerful question, *what kind of person are you becoming in your relationships—and what will remain when you're no longer in the room?*

## The Pillars of a Relationship Legacy
Legacies aren't built in moments of spotlight—they're built in patterns. Not in the rare, grand gestures, but in the small, repeated choices that shape how others experience us over time.

### Consistency: The Quiet Power of Showing Up
Most people don't remember everything you said. But they remember if you said you'd be there—and you were. They remember if you followed through. They remember the text on a hard day, the walk when they didn't want to talk, the ride home when they didn't want to ask.

One of my students once said, "My dad never gave big speeches. But every time I had a soccer game—no matter how early—he was there. Same corner of the bleachers. Same quiet smile. That's how I knew I mattered."

That's consistency. It doesn't always get praise. It doesn't trend. But it stays. And people remember it far longer than anything flashy. When you consistently choose to check in, to listen, to follow through, you become safe. Predictable in the best possible way. You become the kind of person others can build trust with—not just once, but over a lifetime.

### Communication: The Art of Being Present and Real
Words are powerful. They can wound or heal. They can dismiss or validate. They can change someone's day—or their entire sense of self.

I once watched a student gather the courage to tell their roommate, "I know I've been distant. It's not about you. I've been struggling, and I didn't know how to say it." That moment of honesty changed the entire trajectory of their friendship. What could have turned into resentment became an opening for empathy. Not because everything was fixed—but because something honest had been named.

Mindful communication isn't about having the perfect script. It's about presence. Eye contact. Pausing before reacting. Saying "That makes sense" instead of "You're overreacting." It's about being a better question-asker than advice-giver. It's about remembering that sometimes, the most sacred thing you can say is simply: "I'm here."

The legacy of your communication isn't in how articulate you are. It's in how safe people feel to be fully themselves when they're with you.

### Kindness: The Legacy That Needs No Caption
At the end of your life, people may not remember your achievements, your degrees, or even your cleverness. But they will remember how you made them feel.

Kindness is not weakness. It is clarity. It is choosing to treat people not as they deserve, but as they are capable of becoming. It's generosity without expectation. It's small gestures that cost nothing—but mean everything.

You've seen this, haven't you? The professor who stays after class just to say, "That was a great question." The friend who knows your coffee order. The stranger who holds the door and makes eye contact like you matter. These things aren't magic. But the *feeling* they leave behind often is.

One student told me that after a painful breakup, she started saying one kind thing to someone every day—just to keep her heart open. "I thought I was doing it for them," she said. "But really, it was for me. It made me remember who I wanted to be."

Kindness builds legacy not by shouting, but by whispering again and again: *You are worth care. You are worth gentleness. You are not alone.*

And when enough people hear that whisper—from you, from me, from us—it becomes a voice that echoes far beyond our years.

### Intergenerational Influence
The way we love, argue, trust, or withdraw—it often begins before we ever have language for it. Long before our first romantic relationship, first friendship, or first heartbreak, we're learning how relationships work by watching the people who raise us.

Some of us grew up in homes where love was loud, expressed in hugs, shared meals, and "I'm proud of you" said out loud. Others came from quieter places—where love was there, but hidden in packed lunches or the way someone waited up until we got home. And for others still, the blueprint was messy or broken: filled with tension, silence, absence, or inconsistency.

A student once told me, "I didn't realize until college that I was repeating my dad's way of shutting down. Anytime someone gets close, I pull back just like he does." That moment of recognition didn't fix everything overnight. But it opened the door. It gave her a choice. A chance to rewrite the pattern.

This is the quiet power of intergenerational awareness: it helps us decide what to carry forward—and what to gently set down.

We can carry forward the fierce loyalty of a grandmother who never missed a birthday. The tender persistence of a parent who apologized when they got it wrong. The warmth of a mentor who saw something in us when we didn't yet see it in ourselves.

And we can choose to break cycles, too. To say, "The yelling stops with me." To say, "In this family, we say what we feel without fear." To say, "My kids will know what it means to be hugged every day."

Legacy isn't just about what we leave behind—it's about what we decide to keep carrying.

If you've never had the relationship models you needed, that doesn't mean you're doomed. It means you're called to become the model—for your younger siblings, your friends, your future partner, your future children, or even your inner child. You get to write a new story.

You get to turn a fractured past into a healed future. You get to become the ancestor someone else will thank someday.

## Storytelling as a Legacy Tool

The people we remember most often live on in stories. They're the grandparent whose childhood tales still echo in family dinners. The friend who left behind voice notes that make us laugh through our tears. The mentor whose words come to mind at the exact moment we need them—even after they're gone.

## WE RELATE

Stories are how we preserve love. They're how we pass down values, lessons, and reminders of who we are and what matters most. And unlike facts, stories are sticky. They linger. They root in the heart long after the details fade.

One of my students once told me she'd started writing down memories of her late aunt—little things, like how she'd sing while cooking or her habit of clapping after every good movie. "I don't want to forget her rhythms," she said. "She was the first person who made me feel really known."

That's legacy lives in the retelling. You don't have to wait until someone's gone to start storytelling, either. In fact, it's often most powerful when shared now—while you still have time to respond, reconnect, and rewrite.

You can start by writing a letter to someone who shaped your relationship values. Tell them what you've learned from them. Or start collecting your own memories, the kind you hope to pass down someday.

If you have kids—or plan to someday—think about what you want them to know about love. About friendship. About forgiveness. Write it down. Record a video. Tell it around a table. These stories will outlive you, in the best way possible.

Because someday, someone will say,
"My mom used to tell me…"
"My friend once taught me…"
"My teacher always said…"

And just like that, your legacy will live on.

**What Will Your Online Presence Say About You?**
In today's world, part of your legacy lives in the digital space. It lives in text threads, old DMs, photo albums stored in the cloud, and the social media memories that resurface every year. But more than that, your digital footprint tells a story—not just about what you did, but about how you treated people.

When someone scrolls through your feed, your comments, your messages—what kind of person will they see?

A few years ago, one of my students came across an old group chat with a friend who had passed away. "I didn't realize how much I needed to see their words," she said. "Reading our conversations brought them back to life for a moment." That's the sacred power of our digital archives. But it also raises a question: what are you leaving behind?

Are your texts honest? Are your messages kind? Are your online interactions building something real, or just filling space?

You don't have to post inspirational content or craft a perfect persona. But you can be intentional. You can use your digital voice to uplift, to encourage, to remind someone that they matter. That too is legacy. Every word, every post, every late-night text—it's all part of the story you're writing. Make it one you'll be proud of.

**Your Legacy Starts Here**
You don't have to change the world to leave something meaningful behind. Most of us won't write history books or trend online or have our names carved into stone. But we will write something—every day, with our words, our presence, our habits, and our choices. And the ink we use is how we make people feel when they're with us.

Legacy isn't a destination. It's not something you arrive at after a long life lived. It's something you build, quietly, piece by piece, in the way you show up now. It's built in the pause before you react. In the kind text that costs you nothing. In the question you ask when someone seems off. It's built in how you handle disappointment, and in the grace you extend when someone gets it wrong.

People won't remember your GPA or your follower count. They might not even remember your best stories. But they will remember how it felt to be around you. They'll remember if you listened like you meant it. If you apologized with your whole chest. If you saw them not for who they pretended to be—but for who they actually were.

And maybe your legacy won't be obvious. Maybe it will take shape in ways you'll never see. The roommate who learned how to trust again because of your consistency. The friend who dared to believe in their voice because you made space for it. The classmate who changed their mind about love because of how gently you loved.

Legacy is less about what you leave *behind* and more about what you build *within*. It's the quiet echo of every small, loving, intentional moment you chose in a world that often encourages distraction, ego, and disconnection.

The good news is that you don't need to wait until you're older, richer, wiser, or more accomplished to start creating a life that matters. You can begin now. Not by overhauling your entire life, but by choosing to ask deeper questions. By choosing to give more honest and authentic answers. By choosing to pause and empathize before reacting. By choosing a moment of courage when silence feels easier.

In every story, every theory, every reflection—you've seen that the quality of your relationships is shaped by the way you speak, listen, respond, and repair.

We hope this book has encouraged you to be more mindful of your relationships and intentional with your communication. We hope to have given you even more reason to prioritize being present for the people you love.

We hope we've made the case that close, satisfying, meaningful relationships aren't just nice to have—they're essential.

If you've found yourself nodding along...
If something in these pages reminded you of who you are or who you want to become...
If you agree that connection isn't just possible—it's worth the effort...

Well then—

# WE RELATE

We relate.

## *Chapter Fifteen Reflection Questions*

1. Who is in your life right now that makes you feel seen, safe, and valued—and what specific moments or actions have contributed to that feeling? What would it look like to offer that feeling to someone this week?
2. Think about the relationships modeled for you growing up. What communication patterns or emotional habits have you inherited—and which ones are you actively working to change or heal?
3. What's one quiet act of consistency you've received from someone (like Mrs. Rose in the story)—and how has that act shaped your view of trust or care?
4. If someone were to scroll through your messages, social media, or group chats five years from now, what kind of person would they come to know? What would stand out in how you treat people digitally?
5. What's a story about someone you admire that still shapes how you show up in relationships today? Have you ever shared that story with others or written it down?
6. When you're no longer in a room, how do you hope people describe you? Is there a gap between who you want to be and how you're currently showing up?
7. What do you want future generations such as your siblings, your children, your students to learn from your way of loving, listening, or leading? What do you hope they'll carry forward?
8. What's one "micro-legacy" you could begin today? This could be a habit, ritual, or phrase that could quietly impact someone's life over time.
9. Have you ever felt the healing power of someone's kindness in a small moment? What happened, and how did it shift your perspective?
10. Legacy is built in the ordinary. What do your daily habits, reactions, and conversations say about what (and who) you value most?

## *Chapter Fifteen Challenge*

**Relationship Legacy Manifesto: Create a personal philosophy for the way you want to relate today, tomorrow, and beyond.**

Over the past fifteen chapters, you've traveled through the landscape of human connection: from childhood bonds and first friendships to conflict, forgiveness, heartbreak, healing, joy, grief, technology, change, and legacy. You've encountered research, real-life stories, pop culture, and psychology. You've reflected on who you are in relationships and who you want to become.

Now, it's time to bring it all together. This final project invites you to write your *Relationship Legacy Manifesto*, a personal document that articulates the kind of relational life you want to live. It's not about perfection. It's about intention. It's about naming the values, boundaries, and habits that will shape the way you show up for others and for yourself.

**What It Is:** A short-written manifesto (1–2 pages) that combines your personal insights with the major themes of this book. You may write it in narrative form, list format, or as a series of declarations.

### What It's For:
- To give yourself a compass in future relationships
- To reflect on who and how you want to be remembered
- To name what you're letting go of—and what you're building next

*Prompts to Guide You:*
**Self-Awareness & Identity**
- In relationships, I often show up as someone who…
- I've outgrown the belief that I am…
- I want to rewrite my self-talk to reflect…

**Conflict & Repair**
- When things get hard, I want to be the kind of person who…
- I will strive to fight fair by…
- I believe healing begins when…

**Boundaries & Growth**
- I will protect my peace by…
- I've learned to say no when…
- I will let go of guilt when I need to…

**Gratitude, Joy & Emotional Health**
- I will nurture joy by…
- I will practice presence through…
- I will choose gratitude even when…

**Digital Life & Real-World Presence**
- My digital legacy will reflect…
- I want to be known online and in-person for…
- I will be mindful of how I…

**Legacy & Long-Term Impact**
- When people speak about me, I hope they say…
- I want to be remembered for the way I…
- I hope my relationships feel like…

***Your Mission:***
Write your Relationship Legacy Manifesto. Use the prompts above or choose your own. If it helps, start with: *"My relationship legacy begins with…"*

And let that sentence carry you forward. You can write it in a letter to your future self, to someone you love, or just for fun.

# WE RELATE

# APPENDICES

# APPENDIX A: *Knowing Your Interpersonal Communication Competence*

Here are some statements about how people interact with other people. For each statement, choose the response that best reflects YOUR communication with others.

Be honest in your responses and reflect on your communication behavior very carefully. In your responses, use the scale provided below to indicate how well each statement describes YOUR communication.

**ALMOST ALWAYS = 5**
**OFTEN = 4**
**SOMETIMES = 3**
**SELDOM = 2**
**ALMOST NEVER = 1**

_____ 1. I allow friends to see who I really am.

_____ 2. Other people know what I'm thinking.

_____ 3. I reveal how I feel to others.

_____ 4. I can put myself in others' shoes.

_____ 5. I don't know exactly what others are feeling.

_____ 6. Other people think that I understand them.

_____ 7. I am comfortable in social situations.

_____ 8. I feel relaxed in small group gatherings.

_____ 9. I feel insecure in groups of strangers.

_____ 10. When I've been wronged, I confront the person who wronged me.

_____ 11. I have trouble standing up for myself.

_____ 12. I stand up for my rights.

_____ 13. My conversations are one-sided.

_____ 14. I let others know that I understand what they say.

_____ 15. My mind wanders during conversations.

_____ 16. My conversations are characterized by smooth shifts from one topic to the next.

_____ 17. I take charge of conversations I'm in by negotiating what topics we talk about.

_____ 18. In conversations with friends, I perceive not only what they say but what they **don't** say.

_____ 19. My friends can tell when I'm happy or sad.

_____ 20. It isn't easy to find the right words to express myself.

_____ 21. I express myself well verbally.

_____ 22. My communication is typically descriptive, rather than evaluative.

_____ 23. I communicate with others as if they were my equals.

_____ 24. Others would describe me as warm.

_____ 25. My friends truly believe that I care about them.

_____ 26. I try to look others in the eye when I speak with them.

_____ 27. I tell people when I feel close to them.

_____ 28. I accomplish my communication goals.

_____ 29. I can persuade others to my position.

_____ 30. I have trouble convincing others to do what I want them to do.

## *Scoring the Communication Competence Scale*

The items on the scale fall into groups (statistically referred to as factors). The groups are:

**SELF-DISCLOSURE** (alpha = .63)
1. I allow friends to see who I really am.
2. Other people know what I'm thinking.
3. I reveal how I feel to others.

**EMPATHY** (alpha = .49)
4. I can put myself in others' shoes.
5. I don't know exactly what others are feeling. *(R)*
6. Other people think that I understand them.

**SOCIAL RELAXATION** (alpha = .63)
7. I am comfortable in social situations.
8. I feel relaxed in small group gatherings.
9. I feel insecure in groups of strangers. *(R)*

**ASSERTIVENESS** (alpha = .72)
10. When I've been wronged, I confront the person who wronged me.
11. I have trouble standing up for myself. *(R)*
12. I stand up for my rights.

**ALTERCENTRISM** (alpha = .49)
13. My conversations are pretty one-sided. *(R)*
14. I let others know that I understand what they say.
15. My mind wanders during conversations.

**INTERACTION MANAGEMENT** (alpha = .41)
16. My conversations are characterized by smooth shifts…
17. I take charge of conversations I'm in by negotiating…
18. In conversations with friends, I perceive not only what they say…

**EXPRESSIVENESS** (alpha = .46)
19. My friends can tell when I'm happy or sad.
20. It's difficult to find the right words to express myself. *(R)*
21. I express myself well verbally.

**SUPPORTIVENESS** (alpha = .43)
22. My communication is usually descriptive, not evaluative.
23. I communicate with others as though they're equals.
24. Others would describe me as warm.

**IMMEDIACY** (alpha = .45)
25. My friends truly believe that I care about them.
26. I try to look others in the eye when I speak with them.
27. I tell people when I feel close to them.

**ENVIRONMENTAL CONTROL** (alpha = .60)
28. I accomplish my communication goals.
29. I can persuade others to my position.
30. I have trouble convincing others to do what I want them to do. *(R)*

## To get your score:

1) Add up the items under each heading
   a) For example, you would get a *supportiveness* scale by adding items 22, 23, and 24 only.
   b) Any question above that has (R) after it means that it is *reverse scored*. For those items:
      i) $5 = 1$
      ii) $4 = 2$
      iii) $3 = 3$
      iv) $2 = 4$
      v) $1 = 5$

2) With the above in mind, calculate a "Self-score" based on your own responses.
3) Record your scores on the previous page alongside each factor, e.g., "self-disclosure," "empathy," etc.

*Special thanks to Matthew Martin for developing this scale and to my friend Sean Horan for sharing his class assignment with me!*

## APPENDIX B: *The 36 Questions to Fall in Love – Can Intimacy Be Engineered?*

In 1997, psychologist Dr. Arthur Aron and his colleagues at Stony Brook University published a study that has since become a cultural phenomenon. Their research explored whether two people—complete strangers—could accelerate emotional intimacy simply by engaging in a structured conversation. The result led to a a carefully sequenced list of 36 questions, followed by four minutes of sustained eye contact.

The study wasn't originally designed to make people fall in love, despite the romantic framing it's received over the years. Instead, it was intended to test a theory in social psychology: that mutual vulnerability fosters closeness. And it worked. One pair from the original study eventually got married.

These questions, now widely shared, are divided into three sets, each one becoming gradually more personal. They begin with curiosity (e.g., *"Given the choice of anyone in the world, whom would you want as a dinner guest?"*), move through reflection (e.g., *"What do you value most in a friendship?"*), and culminate in emotional risk-taking (e.g., *"Share a personal problem and ask your partner's advice on how they might handle it."*).

When used with intentionality, the questions are disarming. They break through small talk and posturing. They ask us to see and be seen.

Whether you're dating, married, reconnecting with an old friend, or trying to deepen the relationship you have with yourself, the structure of these questions reminds us of something essential: intentional conversation creates space for connection.

And connection, as we've said throughout this book, is not just a nice-to-have. It's why we're here.

Are you ready to find out whether 36 questions lead to love? If so, try it for yourself.

## *How to do the "36 Questions to Fall in Love" activity:*

- Identify someone with whom you'd like to become closer. It could be someone you know well or someone you're just getting to know. Although this exercise has a reputation for making people fall in love, it is actually useful for anyone you want to feel close to, including family members, friends, and acquaintances. Before trying it, make sure both you and your partner are comfortable with sharing personal thoughts and feelings with each other.
- Find a time when you and your partner have at least 45 minutes free and are able to meet in person.
- For 15 minutes, take turns asking one another the questions in Set I below. Each person should answer each question, but in an alternating order, so that a different person goes first each time.
- After 15 minutes, move on to Set II, even if you haven't yet finished the Set I questions. Then spend 15 minutes on Set II, following the same system.
- After 15 minutes on Set II, spend 15 minutes on Set III. (Note: Each set of questions is designed to be more probing than the previous one. The 15-minute periods ensure that you spend an equivalent amount of time at each level of self-disclosure).

### Set I
1. Given the choice of anyone in the world, whom would you want as a dinner guest?
2. Would you like to be famous? In what way?
3. Before making a telephone call, do you ever rehearse what you are going to say? Why?
4. What would constitute a "perfect" day for you?
5. When did you last sing to yourself? To someone else?
6. If you were able to live to the age of 90 and retain either the mind or body of a 30-year-old for the last 60 years of your life, which would you want?
7. Do you have a secret hunch about how you will die?
8. Name three things you and your partner appear to have in common.
9. For what in your life do you feel most grateful?
10. If you could change anything about the way you were raised, what would it be?
11. Take four minutes and tell your partner your life story in as much detail as possible.
12. If you could wake up tomorrow having gained any one quality or ability, what would it be?

### Set II
13. If a crystal ball could tell you the truth about yourself, your life, the future, or anything else, what would you want to know?
14. Is there something that you've dreamed of doing for a long time? Why haven't you done it?
15. What is the greatest accomplishment of your life?
16. What do you value most in a friendship?

17. What is your most treasured memory?
18. What is your most terrible memory?
19. If you knew that in one year you would die suddenly, would you change anything about the way you are now living? Why?
20. What does friendship mean to you?
21. What roles do love and affection play in your life?
22. Alternate sharing something you consider a positive characteristic of your partner. Share a total of five items.
23. How close and warm is your family? Do you feel your childhood was happier than most other people's?
24. How do you feel about your relationship with your mother?

**Set III**

25. Make three true "we" statements each. For instance, "We are both in this room feeling…"
26. Complete this sentence: "I wish I had someone with whom I could share…"
27. If you were going to become a close friend with your partner, please share what would be important for them to know.
28. Tell your partner what you like about them; be very honest this time, saying things that you might not say to someone you've just met.
29. Share with your partner an embarrassing moment in your life.
30. When did you last cry in front of another person? By yourself?
31. Tell your partner something that you like about them [already].
32. What, if anything, is too serious to be joked about?
33. If you were to die this evening with no opportunity to communicate with anyone, what would you most regret not having told someone? Why haven't you told them yet?
34. Your house, containing everything you own, catches fire. After saving your loved ones and pets, you have time to safely make a final dash to save any one item. What would it be? Why?
35. Of all the people in your family, whose death would you find most disturbing? Why?
36. Share a personal problem and ask your partner's advice on how they might handle it. Also, ask your partner to reflect back to you how you seem to be feeling about the problem you have chosen.

You can try this activity with different people you want to develop a deeper connection with—but if your answers start to feel routine, consider making up your own list of questions that become increasingly more personal.

Aron, A., Melinat, E., Aron, E. N., Vallone, R. D., & Bator, R. J. (1997). The experimental generation of interpersonal closeness: A procedure and some preliminary findings. *Personality and Social Psychology Bulletin, 23*(4), 363-377.

# ABOUT THE AUTHORS

 Dr. Trey Guinn is a Professor of Communication Arts and is Assistant Dean for the School of Media and Design at the University of the Incarnate Word in San Antonio, Texas, USA. He is also a Business Communication Specialist for the University of Texas at Austin and a Communication Coach with the McCombs School of Business. His teaching and research are focused primarily on communication effectiveness and human relationships.

As a sought-after author, speaker, facilitator, and executive coach, Trey helps people achieve their goals and master communication skills. He frequently works with groups and professionals across the globe from companies such as Accenture, Amazon, American Express, Apple, AT&T, Bain, BBVA-Compass, BCG, Chevron, Deloitte, Dell, Facebook, Google, Harvard Business School, Intel, Intuit, GE, HP, McKinsey, Microsoft, PWC, Salesforce, Shell, Snap, United States Air Force, and more.

Trey earned his bachelor's and master's degrees from Baylor University and his Ph.D. from the University of Texas at Austin. His scholarship has been presented and published internationally. He remains actively involved with numerous academic organizations and is the immediate past president of the Fulbright Association San Antonio chapter.

Guinn is also an award-winning actor, avid runner, and kitchen experimenter. Most importantly, Trey is the husband to Shannon and dad to three incredible kids. The Guinn family resides in Alamo Heights, Texas, USA, where they can often be spotted walking the neighborhood and playing in the park. His recent book, *Communication Essentials: The Tools You Need to Master Every Type of Professional Interaction,* was published by McGraw-Hill in 2023 and is now available for paperback, e-book, and audiobook!

# ABOUT THE AUTHORS

Dr. Sarah Varga is a current lecturer in the Department of Communication at Baylor University. She teaches undergraduate and graduate courses in interpersonal communication, nonverbal communication, and professional communication. Outside of the classroom, Sarah works as a communication coach for students and professionals at all career stages. Sarah finds great purpose in developing authentic and meaningful personal and professional relationships and helping others do the same.

Sarah is a "Baylor Bear" at heart but had the opportunity to earn degrees from three incredible universities. She earned her bachelor's degree in Theatre Arts from Texas A&M University, her master's degree in communication studies from Baylor University, and her doctorate in communication studies from the University of Texas at Austin.

As the sign in her office says, Sarah aims to "collect moments not things," so she spends as much time as possible with those she loves! You will likely find her with her husband and best friend, Josef, and their four sweet and seriously cool kids. Together with their dog, Mozart or "Mozzie," they enjoy being active outdoors and in, reading all sorts of fiction, enjoying the fine arts, including food in every activity, making up songs about everything, and laughing…a lot.

Made in the USA
Coppell, TX
14 January 2026

67900566R00174